Approaches to learning and teaching

Art &
Design

a toolkit for international teachers

Rachel Logan

T0384565

Series Editors: Paul Ellis and Lauren Harris

CAMBRIDGE
UNIVERSITY PRESS

Shaftesbury Road, Cambridge CB2 8EA, United Kingdom

One Liberty Plaza, 20th Floor, New York, NY 10006, USA

477 Williamstown Road, Port Melbourne, VIC 3207, Australia

314–321, 3rd Floor, Plot 3, Splendor Forum, Jasola District Centre, New Delhi – 110025, India

103 Penang Road, #05–06/07, Visioncrest Commercial, Singapore 238467

Cambridge University Press is part of the University of Cambridge.

It furthers the University's mission by disseminating knowledge in the pursuit of education, learning and research at the highest international levels of excellence.

www.cambridge.org
Information on this title: www.cambridge.org/9781108439848 (Paperback)

© Cambridge Assessment International Education 2018

® IGCSE is a registered trademark

First published 2018

20 19 18 17 16 15 14 13 12 11 10 9

Printed in Great Britain by CPI Group (UK) Ltd, Croydon CR0 4YY

A catalogue record for this publication is available from the British Library

ISBN 978-1-108-43984-8 Paperback

Contents

Online assignment templates and lesson ideas for this book can be found at cambridge.org/go

Acknowledgements

The authors and publishers acknowledge the following sources of copyright material and are grateful for the permissions granted. While every effort has been made, it has not always been possible to identify the sources of all the material used, or to trace all copyright holders. If any omissions are brought to our notice, we will be happy to include the appropriate acknowledgements on reprinting.

Thanks to the following for permission to reproduce images:

Cover image bgblue/Getty Images *Inside in order of appearance* Rachel Logan, Laura Braisher/Getty Images, Ruth Jenkinson/Getty Images, Thomas Samson/AFP/Getty Images; *Images within lesson idea 9* Rachel Logan

Introduction to the series by the editors

1

1 Approaches to learning and teaching Art & Design

This series of books is the result of close collaboration between Cambridge University Press and Cambridge Assessment International Education, both departments of the University of Cambridge. The books are intended as a companion guide for teachers, to supplement your learning and provide you with extra resources for the lessons you are planning. Their focus is deliberately not syllabus-specific, although occasional reference has been made to programmes and qualifications. We want to invite you to set aside for a while assessment objectives and grading, and take the opportunity instead to look in more depth at how you teach your subject and how you motivate and engage with your students.

The themes presented in these books are informed by evidence-based research into what works to improve students' learning and pedagogical best practices. To ensure that these books are first and foremost practical resources, we have chosen not to include too many academic references, but we have provided some suggestions for further reading.

We have further enhanced the books by asking the authors to create accompanying lesson ideas. These are described in the text and can be found in a dedicated space online. We hope the books will become a dynamic and valid representation of what is happening now in learning and teaching in the context in which you work.

Our organisations also offer a wide range of professional development opportunities for teachers. These range from syllabus- and topic-specific workshops and large-scale conferences to suites of accredited qualifications for teachers and school leaders. Our aim is to provide you with valuable support, to build communities and networks, and to help you both enrich your own teaching methodology and evaluate its impact on your students.

Each of the books in this series follows a similar structure. In the third chapter, we have asked our authors to consider the essential elements of their subject, the main concepts that might be covered in a school curriculum, and why these are important. The next chapters give you a brief guide on how to interpret a syllabus or subject guide, and how to plan a programme of study. The authors will encourage you to think too about what is not contained in a syllabus and how you can pass on your own passion for the subject you teach.

The main body of the text takes you through those aspects of learning and teaching which are widely recognised as important. We would like to stress that there is no single recipe for excellent teaching, and that different schools, operating in different countries and cultures, will have strong traditions that should be respected. There is a growing consensus, however, about some important practices and approaches that need to be adopted if students are going to fulfil their potential and be prepared for modern life.

In the common introduction to each of these chapters, we look at what the research says and the benefits and challenges of particular approaches. Each author then focuses on how to translate theory into practice in the context of their subject, offering practical lesson ideas and teacher tips. These chapters are not mutually exclusive but can be read independently of each other and in whichever order suits you best. They form a coherent whole but are presented in such a way that you can dip into the book when and where it is most convenient for you to do so.

The final two chapters are common to all the books in this series and are not written by the subject authors. After the subject context chapters, we include guidance on how to reflect on your teaching and some avenues you might explore to develop your own professional learning. Schools and educational organisations are increasingly interested in the impact that classroom practice has on student outcomes. We have therefore included an exploration of this topic and some practical advice on how to evaluate the success of the learning opportunities you are providing for your students.

We hope you find these books accessible and useful. We have tried to make them conversational in tone so you feel we are sharing good practice rather than directing it. Above all, we hope that the books will inspire you and enable you to think in more depth about how you teach and how your students learn.

Paul Ellis and Lauren Harris

Series Editors

2 Purpose and context

International research into educational effectiveness tells us that student achievement is influenced most by what teachers do in classrooms. In a world of rankings and league tables we tend to notice performance, not preparation, yet the product of education is more than just examinations and certification. Education is also about the formation of effective learning habits that are crucial for success within and beyond the taught curriculum.

The purpose of this series of books is to inspire you as a teacher to reflect on your practice, try new approaches and better understand how to help your students learn. We aim to help you develop your teaching so that your students are prepared for the next level of their education as well as life in the modern world.

This book will encourage you to examine the processes of learning and teaching, not just the outcomes. We will explore a variety of teaching strategies to enable you to select which is most appropriate for your students and the context in which you teach. When you are making your choice, involve your students: all the ideas presented in this book will work best if you engage your students, listen to what they have to say, and consistently evaluate their needs.

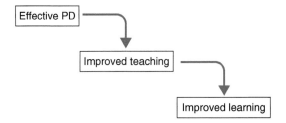

Cognitive psychologists, coaches and sports writers have noted how the aggregation of small changes can lead to success at the highest level. As teachers, we can help our students make marginal gains by guiding them in their learning, encouraging them to think and talk about how they are learning, and giving them the tools to monitor their success. If you take care of the learning, the performance will take care of itself.

When approaching an activity for the first time, or revisiting an area of learning, ask yourself if your students know how to:

- approach a new task and plan which strategies they will use
- monitor their progress and adapt their approach if necessary
- look back and reflect on how well they did and what they might do differently next time.

2 Approaches to learning and teaching Art & Design

Effective students understand that learning is an active process. We need to challenge and stretch our students and enable them to interrogate, analyse and evaluate what they see and hear. Consider whether your students:

- challenge assumptions and ask questions
- try new ideas and take intellectual risks
- devise strategies to overcome any barriers to their learning that they encounter.

As we discuss in Chapter 6 **Active learning** and Chapter 8 **Metacognition**, it is our role as teachers to encourage these practices with our students so that they become established routines. We can help students review their own progress as well as getting a snapshot ourselves of how far they are progressing by using some of the methods we explore in Chapter 7 on **Assessment for Learning**.

Students often view the subject lessons they are attending as separate from each other, but they can gain a great deal if we encourage them to take a more holistic appreciation of what they are learning. This requires not only understanding how various concepts in a subject fit together, but also how to make connections between different areas of knowledge and how to transfer skills from one discipline to another. As our students successfully integrate disciplinary knowledge, they are better able to solve complex problems, generate new ideas and interpret the world around them.

In order for students to construct an understanding of the world and their significance in it, we need to lead students into thinking habitually about why a topic is important on a personal, local and global scale. Do they realise the implications of what they are learning and what they do with their knowledge and skills, not only for themselves but also for their neighbours and the wider world? To what extent can they recognise and express their own perspective as well as the perspectives of others? We will consider how to foster local and global awareness, as well as personal and social responsibility, in Chapter 12 on **Global thinking**.

As part of the learning process, some students will discover barriers to their learning: we need to recognise these and help students to overcome them. Even students who regularly meet success face their own challenges. We have all experienced barriers to our own learning at some point in our lives and should be able as teachers to empathise and share our own methods for dealing with these.

In Chapter 10 **Inclusive education** we discuss how to make learning accessible for everyone and how to ensure that all students receive the instruction and support they need to succeed as students.

Some students are learning through the medium of English when it is not their first language, while others may struggle to understand subject jargon even if they might otherwise appear fluent. For all students, whether they are learning through their first language or an additional language, language is a vehicle for learning. It is through language that students access the content of the lesson and communicate their ideas. So, as teachers, it is our responsibility to make sure that language isn't a barrier to learning. In Chapter 9 on **Language awareness** we look at how teachers can pay closer attention to language to ensure that all students can access the content of a lesson.

Alongside a greater understanding of what works in education and why, we (as teachers) can also seek to improve how we teach and expand the tools we have at our disposal. For this reason, we have included Chapter 11 **Teaching with digital technologies**, discussing what this means for our classrooms and for us as teachers. Institutes of higher education and employers want to work with students who are effective communicators and who are information literate. Technology brings both advantages and challenges and we invite you to reflect on how to use it appropriately.

This book has been written to help you think harder about the impact of your teaching on your students' learning. It is up to you to set an example for your students and to provide them with opportunities to celebrate success, learn from failure and, ultimately, to succeed.

We hope you will share what you gain from this book with other teachers and that you will be inspired by the ideas that are presented here. We hope that you will encourage your school leaders to foster a positive environment that allows both you and your students to meet with success and to learn from mistakes when success is not immediate. We hope too that this book can help in the creation and continuation of a culture where learning and teaching are valued and through which we can discover together what works best for each and every one of our students.

3 | The nature of the subject

The scope of Art and Design

A broad arts experience is important at the beginning of secondary level learning, so that students have a working vocabulary of art techniques and processes to develop if they go on to further study. This can be taught as lots of short projects in a range of different materials and pathways. Younger students often want to finish something, and feel uneasy with expressive or explorative work where they aren't sure what's required of them – this is where a really well-written project brief is useful. With older students heading into their exam years, you would expect them to be able to plan and develop their own projects within a given title or context, but in order to be able to do this they have to be taught to work like that right from the start of their secondary studies.

Art and Design can encompass so many different materials, tools and techniques that it can be difficult to know where to begin when planning what to teach. For example, the history of art is the history of time and civilisation, so it can be overwhelming when you want to know where to start planning. What you are really teaching is a way of communicating, of expressing meaning without words and a way of developing ideas towards an outcome. Most students will have had some form of Art and Design learning in their primary studies, but not everyone. Some will have a natural fluency and pick things up quickly, while others will have to work a bit harder at it, just like every subject.

Teaching large groups

At secondary level, some schools will offer Art and Design to all their students as part of the curriculum, while others might offer it only to those students who want to go on and take an exam or qualification. In a large school where everyone studies Art and Design, there can be several different groups all taking different pathways. For example, the most popular are painting and drawing, fashion and textiles, and graphics and photography. Within these you might have several ability groups and more than one teacher to internally assess, plan projects and look after resources.

Large groups mean that you can have lots of project work with idea sharing and peer assessment. Sometimes there isn't time to teach lots of new techniques, or focus on developing ideas and skills, so you may need to build in time for skills workshops and short projects that focus on a particular technique. In a larger group, it can be more difficult to find the time to give each student individual feedback about how their projects are progressing, or to listen to them talking through their ideas. This is where peer review and self-evaluation can really be effective teaching strategies.

Teacher Tip

Development tasks and ideas generation can be a great way of creating aspirational projects when you don't have lots of resources. Start with a review of some existing objects and set a design challenge.

LESSON IDEA 3.1: SETTING A DESIGN CHALLENGE
Generating and developing ideas is one of the main skills to develop in Art and Design. A great way to start is by looking at existing products and thinking about how they can be improved. Packaging products are useful examples as they are easy to get hold of, colourful and often made in an interesting way. Ask each student to bring in the empty packaging of a product, for example a shampoo bottle, and then redesign the packaging, including drawing, photography and modelling.

Teaching small groups

Many schools just have one Art and Design teacher, and those schools with small groups might find that the teacher has to become an expert in a wide range of subjects to cater for the broad demands of their students. Students enjoy finding out about artists and techniques that their teacher doesn't know about – you really can't know everything or every artist. Being able to encourage students to find out about different artists and techniques is a very important part of Art and Design teaching; one of the things I enjoy most about teaching is learning new things from my students. This is great for the older students, but empowering younger students to manage their own learning is a skill in itself. As a teacher, you might find yourself constantly learning new things. My own specialism is three-dimensional design, but I have spent many years teaching drawing, photography, graphics and textiles. This experience has given me the confidence to teach with a broad range of materials and techniques, and to allow creative crossovers between pathways. In fact, I would now say that I don't teach Art and Design, I teach creative problem-solving and design thinking.

Teaching transferable skills

Not every student you teach will become an artist or embark on a career in the Art and Design industry. However, with access to a broad range of art experiences, some of those students will make a connection with something that they can turn into a lifelong career. Art and Design is one of the largest industries, with enormous potential for employment globally. Not only that, it's important for giving students a means of expression and self-reflection. Different viewpoints can be explored, demonstrating empathy.

Figure 3.1: The benefits of studying Art and Design.

Presentation skills are an important part of Art and Design, and these skills can help improve the way that work for other subjects is finished and presented. This doesn't just mean in terms of neatness; this also relates to the way students present themselves and articulate their ideas in person before the rest of the class. Having students talk about ideas and how their work has developed is part of Art and Design learning, and builds self-confidence.

Developing creative thinkers

Art and Design students can be taught to develop their creative thinking and problem-solving skills; these transferable skills can be used in their creative writing, literature and history studies. Creative problem solvers break the challenge down into portions or stages, and define what needs to be done and why. Then they look for ways of resolving the problem and evaluate their ideas as they work. This iterative way of working can be applied to academic subjects, as well as practical Art and Design projects. These types of skills have a positive impact on other areas of study and on students' ability to manage their own learning. Access to music, art and drama in the early years of schooling can also help students engage with their environments and actually enjoy their learning.

Teacher Tip

Lesson idea 9.2 is a template for comparing artworks. You can use this list to create a visual timeline and make links with the history teacher to look for ways to help your students explore context. Students could pick two of the artists whose lives would have overlapped, and look at historical events that they might have lived through to see if they had an impact on their lives. For example, were they growing up during a period of conflict? Could they have been inspired by one of the other artists' work? Were there any technological advancements that might have affected their work, such as new materials/technology, or the birth of photography?

Creative subjects work best with project style learning, and can give opportunities for cross-curricular learning and joined up thinking. The *Bridges* project introduced in this chapter (full assignment online) shows how an idea can be explored through a range of different mediums and techniques, and this project could be used as a template for your own projects. It could be worth looking for ways to link up with other topics being taught at the same time, so find out what's being taught in history or science that could lead to a joint project. For example, a creative project with science could be based on looking at cells through microscopes, and then drawing images of cells and scaling them up into large semi-abstract paintings.

Teacher Tip

As a teacher, it's useful to be reflective about your own skills, and this is something you can also encourage in your students. One way is by doing a skills audit. You could do this with your students at the start of the year as a way of introducing them to managing their own learning and improvement. This could be a written task that they do in their sketchbook, or something that you ask them to do in pairs, talking about their answers.

Questions to ask yourself:

- What am I good at?
  - Sample answers: *Drawing, remembering artists' names, talking about my ideas.*
- What do I need a bit of help with?
  - Sample answers: *Painting, mixing colours.*
- What do I not feel confident with?
  - Sample answers: *Spelling, taking notes.*
- Where can I get help/what can I do to improve?
  - Sample answers: *Practise, watch tutorials, read about artists and take notes in my sketchbook.*

What do the Cambridge Learner attributes look like in an Art and Design student?

It's important to consider what sort of skills and personal qualities you are hoping to develop in your students. Their learning experience isn't just about how good at drawing they become, it's about how they develop as people, and engage with lifelong learning and self-improvement. In an Art and Design student, these personal attributes can be seen in the following ways:

- **Communication** – being able to express meaning visually through drawings, colours and imagery; sharing and discussing ideas with other colleagues, giving and receiving feedback; collaborating to meet deadlines and shared goals, share resources and help each other.
- **Creativity** – being investigative and exploring materials; testing things out to see if they work; trying new ideas when things don't work out as planned; looking for new ways of solving problems and being imaginative; being careful with resources to make the most of them.
- **Reflection** – being able to evaluate and comment on own performance; being able to discuss ideas and thought processes both verbally and by using evaluative annotation; adapting ideas in response to feedback and not being afraid to change things.
- **Confidence** – this can be confidence with materials and techniques, self-confidence in own skills, and confidence when presenting ideas to the class or a teacher. A confident student is happy to use the correct specialist language when talking or writing about how their ideas evolved.
- **Engagement** – involvement in own learning with an active approach; able to self-monitor progress and manage time. An engaged student looks for things outside school that are related to their work, reads around the subject and practises at home without being asked.
- **Innovation** – enjoys developing skills to solve problems creatively; interested in new ways of looking at things, or working and putting materials together in a fresh way.

Subjective or objective?

I often hear it said that art is hard to assess because it's so subjective, or that there are no right or wrong answers in art. Those statements just aren't true and are something that Art and Design teachers have to challenge regularly. When Art and Design work is being assessed, it is the objective process of idea generation and resolution that is being assessed, along with technical competencies based around the development of the idea and the use of appropriate materials and techniques. There are definitely wrong answers in Art and Design, just as there are in other subjects. There are ideas that don't work or projects that run out of time, but more often it's because they have been poorly resolved and not properly developed.

Sometimes when things take an unexpected turn, interesting new options open up, and your students should be excited about these new possibilities. If you were teaching science, you would expect students to test things out and analyse their results; art is just the same. Creative writing in literature lessons, music and drama have that same quality of the students' own personal expression, which is to be encouraged, but they still have a set of technical requirements and levels of competency to achieve in order to be able to progress in the subject. You might have an idea of what you want your students to learn, but you also need to be able to help them make choices and resolve ideas that don't always work first time. Planning a course is not just about what you are going to teach them, but what they are going to do in order to learn.

The *Bridges* project

The *Bridges* project (online) is a 4-week project that introduces students to researching and developing their ideas, and combining new technical skills with creative ideas development. In later chapters, references to the *Bridges* project show how the different elements can be explored when focusing on different teaching strategies. It can provide a template for assignment briefs that can be tailored to suit your own classes.

Teaching methods used in the *Bridges* project that can be adapted for other projects include:

- Ideas generation
- Exploring ideas creatively and verbally, and through drawings and photographs
- Not over-assessing everything
- To copy or not; learning through copying is useful for some things, but learning to develop ideas is valuable too
- Peer assessment and feedback.

Teacher Tip

Peer learning is a very effective teaching method, and great if you have large groups and not much time. If you have an end of year art show or performance for your older students, why not set a project for your younger students to look round the show, or watch the performance, and then interview some of the older students? They could do a write up for the school website or for a presentation in assembly. The older students will enjoy the experience of talking about their work and it gives the younger students an idea of their goals as they work their way through school.

Example questions can be:

- Where did you get your inspiration?
- What things did you enjoy most?
- What would you do differently if you had to do it again?

You could ask the students to take photos and draw their favourite pieces as part of their project work.

Lesson idea 7.2 explains how you could put this into practice in the classroom.

Teaching tools

Some schools set aside more time for academic subjects, and there might be a school policy not to set homework for certain school years or subjects. But for art, a home sketchbook can be a great way of keeping students engaged between lessons and start to enjoy drawing for pleasure. Lots of students have phones with cameras and are busy recording the world around them – you could capture this enthusiasm with some careful photography projects that would be great homework tasks. Homework that doesn't get checked ends up not getting done, so even if you don't assess everything, it's good practice to regularly check home sketchbooks.

Setting short regular homework tasks that are based around preparing for the next lesson can keep students engaged and enthused. This style of teaching is called 'flipped learning' and is a much more effective use of homework than setting tasks to finish off work started in lessons.

Teacher Tip

Homework ideas that can feed into lessons can be set in the home sketchbook. Short tasks related to project work, such as development of ideas, make relevant homework tasks and get students used to thinking about their art project between classes (e.g. find five different viewpoints or three different colour schemes based on the task covered in class).

☑ **LESSON IDEA ONLINE 3.2: HOME SKETCHBOOK**
Use this lesson idea to encourage students to draw outside school time, and to start to use Art and Design language.

Cultural capital

This is what your students bring with them: it is a collection of all their experiences so far, and each student is different. This is the part of them that they will draw on for the imagination and personal voice that makes each piece of student work different. When studying Art and Design, you will teach your students to take inspiration from things they have experienced as children, their opinions and feelings, and their memories. Cultural capital includes the holidays and family experiences, the school trips, museums, stories and the connections that they make, and it's the home of all their ideas. I'm always amazed that when I'm teaching ceramics and have given everyone the same instructions and a ball of clay from the same bag, I can get thirty different pieces of clay work back. Each student can embrace the same task in a different way, depending on their cultural capital.

3

Approaches to learning and teaching Art & Design

Summary

- Knowing what skills your students already have is key to deciding what you are going to concentrate on during their time with you.

- Think about your own personal strengths in terms of Art and Design, and what resources you have available.

- Being able to encourage your students to draw on their own experiences and interests will help them to engage with their learning and develop projects that can keep them motivated.

Key considerations

4

Practical considerations

Some of the things you will need to consider when teaching Art and Design include practical constraints, such as space, budgets, skills and equipment. Other less tangible considerations that have an impact on students are parental pressure, performance targets, self-esteem and well-being.

One of the key practical considerations for Art and Design is resourcing. Materials and equipment can be expensive, and specialist Art and Design studios need space and light, as well as room for equipment. There are still lots of things you can do on a limited budget or in a small space it just takes a bit of creative problem-solving. Opportunities to collaborate with other curriculum areas should be explored so that students can make links with science, literature and history, which could lead to some really exciting project work.

> ☑ **LESSON IDEA ONLINE 4.1: IMAGINARY CONVERSATIONS**
>
> This lesson idea uses images from Art and Design as a starting point for creative writing. It could form a collaborative project with the English Literature department to help develop vocabulary and creative writing skills, together with visual narrative skills.

Art and Design can give students a visual vocabulary for expressing their emotions because it teaches them to draw on their own memories and feelings, and to use their imagination. It can help them develop empathy by exploring other ways of communicating, understanding different cultures and seeing things from other viewpoints. Producing and making creative work can greatly improve students' self-esteem, build confidence and improve mental health. With all those benefits, suddenly the extra space and resources are worth it!

You make the difference

One of the most important things in your classroom that can make the difference is – you. The way you welcome your students into class and make them feel valued and inspired will set the tone for the lesson. Taking time to show techniques properly, listen to their ideas and ask questions that help them extend their research are all teaching and learning techniques that can help you foster a supportive learning environment. You don't need to know all the answers, but you do need to be able to show your students how to learn and foster a sense of discovery that makes them enjoy their learning.

Teacher Tip

If resources are in short supply, focus on teaching observation and drawing skills. Drawing from still life arrangements in the classroom, or drawing and painting objects from nature and really concentrating on observing the colour, shapes and texture, can be taught with very few resources. Making links with local events and local culture helps students develop their sense of belonging, so explore ways to encourage students to take inspiration from their own environments and experience.

Measuring success

Success comes in many forms; it's not always just measured by high grades. For some students, just coming to school every day might be their idea of success. Your students might think that technical excellence is the mark of success and that they have to produce highly accurate copies of artefacts or other artists' works to be successful. Others might value originality and personal expression. Each school has a different culture, and it will be part of your school ethos to define how success is measured. In some schools, the definition of success is about all students achieving their potential at whatever level they can, while others may be very performance driven.

This is where understanding the syllabus is important – which is covered in more detail in Chapter 5 **Interpreting a syllabus**. This will be your point of reference for what needs to be achieved, and you can then break down successful milestones along the way.

There is a common misconception that a piece of art is only good if you like it. When Art and Design work is being assessed, it is the process of making connections, sourcing and developing ideas towards a resolved outcome that is being judged. Alongside that are levels of technical competence that must be met in order to make progress. Lesson idea 5.3 uses the assessment criteria to help students plan their project towards meeting the assessment objectives. This can be combined with the breakdown of the assessment criteria to help students understand the differing levels of competency each mark band requires. The creative journey being assessed is about the student justifying why they think it's a good idea, what decisions they made along the way to select and refine their work, and the way they added meaning to their final outcome. This opportunity for a creative journey is lost if students are copying a piece of work or working to a very narrow assignment brief.

Teacher Tip

Think about ways to revise stale project briefs to open up the opportunities for idea generation. So instead of a project to create a chess set from recycled materials, it could be a project to design a game made from recycled materials. Suddenly it's much more open and the students need to really think about all the elements that go into a game.

Overcoming obstacles

Parental pressure on students can be a consideration for Art and Design, as some parents may not see the value in this area of study, even if their child wants to continue. They may feel they have to choose a different career in order to get a job. The creative industry is one of the biggest global employers with so many rich and interesting career possibilities. Everything in our lives has been created by art students in one way or another; from the clothes we wear to our houses and all the things we use every day. The digital entertainment industry is the fastest growing industry and relies heavily on creative graduates.

High achieving students often perform highly in art as well, and schools with an inclusive arts-rich curriculum perform well overall. Students who are encouraged to use active learning styles and initiate their own learning have a high level of engagement, and this can have a positive effect on their approach to work in other subjects.

Teacher Tip

Making sure that your Art and Design students have a visible presence in the school can help to raise aspirations and understanding about the value of Art and Design. This is where displays of work in the corridors, and regular exhibitions of student work that parents are invited to, can help overcome the perception that art is an easy subject or leads to limited career choices.

Differentiation

A key consideration is the differing abilities and learning styles of your students. You may have classes of mixed abilities, different paces for learning new techniques, and whole groups all doing different things. It could be tempting to just make everyone produce the same outcome and have a formula that you feel works, but this misses opportunities to meet the assessment objectives for developing ideas, personal voice and expression. It can be hard to distinguish between ability levels when students all produce very similar styles of work. This is where active learning helps to differentiate the tasks, as students are more involved with their own projects, and they tend to be more focused and enjoy work more when they feel a greater sense of ownership over what they are producing. In the next few chapters there are some practical tips that you can use with your students to help them develop self- and peer review skills that will free up teacher time.

When students discuss and share ideas, they motivate each other and build a supportive and successful environment for learning. Keep students motivated by making the project work active, changing the length and focus of different projects, and allowing space and time to learn practical and technical skills. Encourage self-respect by teaching students to take care over the finish of their work. Even simple things like improving presentation can help improve grades: try typing out evaluation comments and printing them onto tracing paper if handwriting isn't neat.

Teacher Tip

Using examples of past work to show students different ways of working can help to define what is expected of them. It doesn't need to be a whole project, but sometimes good examples of spider diagrams, thumbnail sketches, annotation and recording of information can help students to see how these key skills can be approached. It can help motivate students at all ability levels if your examples are from a range of different marks.

LESSON IDEA 4.2: LARGE SCALE SPIDER DIAGRAMS

A great way to capture a lot of information quickly is to tape large sheets of paper together and stick them on a wall to start a giant spider diagram based around a starting point, for example, the *Bridges* project, available online. You could start by asking students to say or write obvious examples of bridges, and then move on to more conceptual ideas, like veins, waterways and synapses. From this you could start talking about materials and construction methods. With this giant spider diagram of ideas, students can start to narrow down areas that they want to start researching and identify what would be a primary and secondary source.

Primary and secondary sources

Something that is fundamental in Art and Design, but often misunderstood by students, is the definition of primary and secondary sources. **Primary sources** mean using first-hand research. First-hand means it's in front of you. It doesn't mean taking a photo of an inanimate object like a tap and then drawing from the photo in the classroom; it means drawing the tap in its location. Some students describe the materials they used first as their primary source, which shows that they have misunderstood what a primary source is. First-hand recording means taking information from the object in front of you – which can be rubbings, photos and drawings.

Figure 4.1: Sketchbooks are useful for students to show how their ideas have developed from research using primary and secondary sources.

Working from a photograph produces a very flat image, but using photographs to help capture details can help inform work. If your students are drawing something in pencil and want to produce a colour study later, taking photos of the colours or details would be useful primary recording. Interviews are great ways of gathering information first-hand, and a case study would be a secondary source. Access to a wide range of art experiences, such as visits to galleries and museums,

Approaches to learning and teaching Art & Design

meeting creative practitioners, and exploring the work of other artists and designers, all add considerable value to Art and Design learning.

Secondary sources are information that has already been processed by somebody, such as articles, webpages and photos that another person has taken. In design-based tasks, it's normal to see what already exists before designing your own product or redeveloping something already in production, so there might be more use of secondary sources initially and then more use of primary sources when developing design work. For fine art, it might be more appropriate to have an interpretative approach to working. Again, this would normally be informed by working from first-hand sources to gather ideas and information, and using secondary sources to explore how other artists have conveyed meaning and expression in their work.

Lesson idea 5.1 is a sample project that starts by working from primary sources and then develops ideas using secondary sources. It shows how students can access a range of different sources of information and inspiration when they are in the early stages of a project. Gathering enough visual information from drawing, observing, and recording objects and ideas related to the theme, can give students enough source material to be able to generate lots of ideas and stay motivated on longer projects.

Summary

Some of the key considerations are practical and can be addressed with careful resource planning, while others involve raising awareness of the high value of Art and Design as part of the curriculum.

Your key considerations include:

- defining what success looks like

- taking stock of what skills and resources you have

- thinking about the different needs of your students

- raising aspirations and the presence of Art and Design within your school through displays, exhibitions and performances

- looking for opportunities to work across subjects to deepen learning

- encouraging students to draw on their own experience, feelings and imagination.

Interpreting a syllabus

Turning a syllabus into a course

For Art and Design, there is so much potential to build a really interesting and creative course that you might wonder how you can fit it all into two years. The syllabus covers a wide range of Art and Design media and techniques, but that doesn't mean that you have to teach everything. It comes back to what resources you have at your school and where your own strengths are. It could also be worth investigating the opportunities for further study and employment in the creative industries in your region, so that you can guide your students towards these and ensure that they have the right skills.

Practical tasks and projects can be more meaningful with external involvement, so look for opportunities to include live projects, visiting speakers, or off-site trips and visits. If you really can't access any of these things you could still use case studies or simulated live briefs – these can be a context or a scenario, as if you had a customer setting a brief.

Teacher Tip

Look for opportunities to give projects a realistic context. Even something as simple as designing a window display for a local shop can bring a realistic element into projects and move away from projects with a narrow focus, such as 'design a poster about healthy living for the school canteen'.

The syllabus is your guide for the type of content that you should teach your students, for detailed information about the nature of the components and the form that the assessment will take. It's a framework that has been developed to support you to build a creative course appropriate for your school and your students. Specimen papers and past papers are a great resource for writing projects and for using as coursework topics. They can really help to frame a project in the style of the exam and get your students used to appropriate language and the type of projects that they will need to do at the end of the course.

Teacher Tip

One way to make learning more meaningful can be to work across curriculum areas and combine resources. There might be a shared topic or starting point that could be used to start a project. This might be a theatre trip or off-site visit, or a topic in another subject that could make an inspiring link with art. For example: exploring artists and materials available during the period covered in a history project; looking at cells through microscopes in science and linking it with an art project based on close-ups, patterns and shapes.

To turn a syllabus into a course you need to really focus on what you want your students to learn and then break it down into portions of learning. By the end of their course, students should be ready to take the exam and feel confident with a range of materials, and they should be able to develop and manage a project that works towards the assessment objectives. A good way to start can be a series of small projects that cover a range of different techniques, materials and processes, and then build up to longer projects that focus more on researching and developing ideas.

Writing a scheme of work

This is a really useful way to break a course down into weekly portions. It can help you plan out the projects and skills that you want to cover over time. Once you have mapped what skill building workshops and projects will take place over the course, you can think about the resources that you need and start to prepare well in advance. If you have several year groups, it can also help you bundle similar tasks together, which can help to cut down on your own preparation time and save resources in terms of ordering materials. (See the *Bridges* online assignment for an example of a scheme of work template.)

Teacher Tip

Look for opportunities to link learning over year groups to save on your preparation time. You might be able to set up a display, plan a trip or invite a guest in that could work for a number of year groups. For example, a display in class of sweets and cakes could be used for the younger year groups to do a painting project based on observation and colour mixing, and could also be a great way to start a project on hyperrealism and abstraction with the older year groups. (See Lesson idea 5.1.)

☑ **LESSON IDEA ONLINE 5.1: A PIECE OF CAKE**

The *A Piece of cake* assignment has been written as a long project that covers a number of different Art and Design areas, including drawing, photography, ceramics, painting and digital manipulation. It has been broken down into eight weekly sessions. You could make the project longer by adding feedback and interim assessments in the lesson, or shorter by taking out the clay work activity.

Use Lesson idea 5.1 Week 1 to introduce the *A Piece of cake* assignment to students.

Laying the foundations

At the start of secondary education for Art and Design, the focus should be on interesting and creative projects, with lots of opportunities for assessment for learning. Project work can be explorative, but often at this level students really like to feel like something is finished, and feel intimidated by lots of open mark making or materials exploration. Open-ended or self-directed projects can be difficult to manage with younger students, so clear directions and expectations will help them to stay on track. Using templates for tasks like recording research or comparing artworks can be useful to encourage learning and a specialist vocabulary. Projects can be a mix of short projects that focus on research or techniques, and longer and more involved projects that lead towards a developed outcome.

Teacher Tip

To keep students engaged, you could set regular challenges like photo competitions, a home sketchbook, or drawing projects to get the students thinking creatively and engaging with Art and Design between lessons. Try basing tasks around topics and encourage links between pathways; for example, a repeat pattern project that could be used as wrapping paper, fabric or the background on a poster. Using past question papers, even for the younger students, can help you to structure projects in the style of the exam format, so students get used to working that way.

The most successful projects have a clear narrative running through them. You can see the starting point in the student's research and then how their idea has unfolded and changed through the development sheets. Annotation and evaluative comments can be really helpful to show what decisions were made, but these don't always need to be written. What is important is to see the journey that the student has made, and the testing and development of their ideas.

Teacher Tip

Circling the chosen images on a contact sheet, putting a tick next to a preferred colour scheme or layout, or even just mounting up a piece of work that has worked really well, all show that the student has gone through a process of selection and refinement, without having to write lots of evaluative comments. Using a highlighter or underlining the parts of a text that were useful when doing research can also show that the student is refining their ideas and making informed judgements about their research as ideas develop.

Embedding skills and building confidence for exams

Year one

Most Art and Design syllabuses cover two years, so in the first year the focus could be on skill building workshops, and a rotation through different pathways such as graphics, fine art, textiles printmaking or three-dimensional design. It's good to mix up short projects and build them into longer and more independent projects. Instead of having each project for half a term or of equal length, there could be short two-week projects that encourage ideas generation, followed by a four-week project that has a well-defined outcome. You could focus on a different aspect each time; for example, a research-rich project, followed by a loose and experimental project, then one where the back up work has to be really well presented along with a finished outcome.

Drawing is a really vital tool for all areas of Art and Design, and often gets neglected in favour of techniques that get quicker results, like taking photos on a phone or using photo-sharing apps for gathering ideas. Drawing is a way of communicating ideas and meaning, but it's also something that can be taught and improves with practice. The focus in the first exam year should be on building confidence with materials and processes, and with researching and developing ideas, so that these skills all improve together in the second year.

Year two

The second year will be dominated by preparing for exams. This is where you might focus on a fully resolved coursework project with supporting studies. The coursework might be the place where you give a bit more guidance on time management and on the development of ideas. You could give the students a selection of possible topics or starting points, rather than every student making similar work, but again this depends on class sizes and resources. This can be done in advance of the exam piece.

The syllabus should help to explain the different nature of components, but often the exam piece is about demonstrating the student's ability to create a resolved piece of work in a given time period, and with a clear starting point. Students also need to be able to demonstrate their time management skills, presentation, annotation and evaluation skills.

Teacher Tip

You might find yourself suddenly taking on an exam group in their final year and not having time to teach them everything you want to cover. Going back to basics with drawing and photography skills can strengthen their exam work by ensuring that they have skills in recording and observing the world around them.

The design cycle

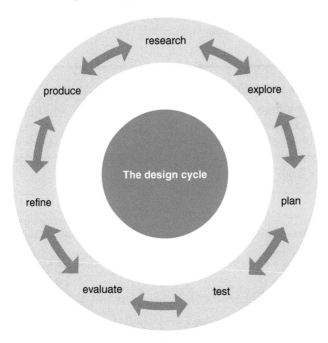

Figure 5.1: The design cycle.

The assessment objectives work well with the design cycle process, so that this becomes the natural workflow for your students. An initial period of exploration around a topic or theme should lead naturally into the research stage. From their research, students might pick one or two areas to investigate in more depth. This can then lead into materials experimentation: exploring which media, techniques and materials would work the best. The design cycle is a process flow and not always linear, so if students come up against a dead end or lose motivation, they should be encouraged to go back into their research and follow one of their other original ideas or areas for research. Evaluation and reflection should be a thread running through a project, rather than something completed at the end. This is an iterative style of working.

Younger or less able older students benefit from templates and worksheets to help structure their ideas, and if you work in this way from the start, as they get older and more confident they should be able to apply the thought process independently without using templates. You are not looking for students to get things right first time, but you want them to try things out and be able to make judgements about what is working and why, and if not, what to do next. Their work should be a series of changes made as a result of feedback, testing or experimentation. (The lesson ideas in Chapter 8 **Metacognition** support this.)

☑ LESSON IDEA ONLINE 5.2: USING SURVEYS

Surveys are a great way to get feedback on ideas or design quickly. This type of activity can help students refocus if they are losing momentum. Gathering feedback from a range of different people can often feel more valuable to the student than just getting feedback from the teacher.

Preparing for skills needed in assessments: breaking down the assessment objectives

The assessment objectives have been written to reflect the kind of workflow used in Art and Design, and the way that people in the creative industries usually work. They should be seen as elements that link together, rather than steps that can be completed on their own. In Art and Design, the assessment objectives are often based around researching, exploring and investigating, developing and then resolving or presenting a resolved idea.

⧉ LESSON IDEA ONLINE 5.3: USING ASSESSMENT CRITERIA FOR PEER ASSESSMENT AND SELF-ASSESSMENT

Peer assessment is a very successful teaching tool. Often, if students set targets for each other, it helps them to focus on what should be done in their own work. Giving and receiving feedback is a valuable part of learning, not just for Art and Design.

Start introducing the language of the assessment criteria early so that students have a better understanding of their longer-term aims for Art and Design assessments.

Teacher Tip

Students should become familiar with the assessment objectives and the criteria that they are going to be marked against. Print the assessment objectives out on big sheets of paper and laminate them, or stick them on the classroom wall. For each project, ask students to write what they think they need to do for each assessment objective. Leave it on the wall in the classroom, and encourage students to add to it as they think of things or complete something that they want to share.

Often what is required isn't just more work but a more skilful use of materials and processes, and more evidence of the decisions and judgements that the student has made as their project develops. This kind of evidence also adds authenticity to the students' work, as it can be seen where their idea came from and how it was developed. When students pick something from the internet and copy it, often they run out of ways to develop it further.

For A Level, the assessment objectives flow on from IGCSE®, but have more critical understanding and a higher level of independent learning. The practical skills should be more sophisticated, but the real difference at the higher levels are thinking skills. This type of skill can be introduced at secondary level and embedded by gently supporting students as they learn, and giving them opportunities to develop ways to be reflective and analytical about their sources and their ideas.

Reflection is one of the core skills to embed in your students. They should be able to discuss what's working and what needs changing, as well as being able to describe what they did.

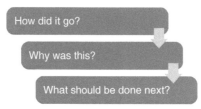

How did it go?

Why was this?

What should be done next?

Figure 5.2: Effective reflection.

As a teacher, reflection is really valuable to your own professional development. You could add a column on your scheme of work or lesson plan for reflection and note down how you feel the session went or what you would do differently next time. Be honest: what worked, and what would you change? It can be hard to judge how long different tasks will take different ability groups, so you can have a few extra tasks in mind for those that work quickly, or a few refocus activities for students that run out of ideas or need help managing their time. If you use reflection to improve your own professional development, it will be easier to encourage reflection as a tool for learning in your students.

☑ LESSON IDEA ONLINE 5.4: SELF-REFLECTION

Use this handy template to introduce self-reflection activities for your students.

Teacher Tip

To develop your own self-reflection skills, you could start a journal about your teaching. It can be notes in your diary, on your lesson plans or schemes of work, or something more detailed. It can give you a space to note down what went well or what you could do differently next time.

Skill building workshops

The kind of skills to develop can be practical skills such as drawing, painting and making; or they can be thinking skills such as generating ideas, problem-solving and evaluating. Skill building can also include encouraging students to make cognitive links between pathways and subjects, and to bring their own voice and interests to their artwork.

Skill building workshops could be based on practical tasks like colour mixing, paint techniques, photography and process-led workshops, such as printmaking, sewing, using software and ceramics. The list goes on, so this is where you need to think about your strengths and the resources available in your school.

Sometimes things don't go as planned, and this is a vital aspect of learning. I photograph my students' work and they are often really happy to be asked. Sometimes, if something goes wrong it can be incredibly useful as a resource to explain what went wrong and why. If handled sensitively, this can often make them feel better about their work not going as planned. We don't always teach students how to learn from mistakes, but if you are building a supportive and open atmosphere in your classroom, they should feel confident sharing their less successful moments.

Summary

- Think about where your students need to be at the end of their studies and what sort of skills they are starting with.

- Be realistic about what you can achieve in the time available, and think about your strengths and what is available in your school.

- Break learning down into portions and into interesting projects. Look for opportunities to combine tasks and preparation to save your time.

- Spend time building up resources so that you have examples of good practice to share with your students. It could be a really thorough mind map or a well-drawn still life. They don't all have to have achieved top marks, but could demonstrate a point really well and be something that students can relate to.

6 | Active learning

What is active learning?

Active learning is a pedagogical practice that places student learning at its centre. It focuses on *how* students learn, not just on *what* they learn. We as teachers need to encourage students to 'think hard', rather than passively receive information. Active learning encourages students to take responsibility for their learning and supports them in becoming independent and confident learners in school and beyond.

Research shows us that it is not possible to transmit understanding to students by simply telling them what they need to know. Instead, we need to make sure that we challenge students' thinking and support them in building their own understanding. Active learning encourages more complex thought processes, such as evaluating, analysing and synthesising, which foster a greater number of neural connections in the brain. While some students may be able to create their own meaning from information received passively, others will not. Active learning enables all students to build knowledge and understanding in response to the opportunities we provide.

Why adopt an active learning approach?

We can enrich all areas of the curriculum, at all stages, by embedding an active learning approach.

In active learning, we need to think not only about the content but also about the process. It gives students greater involvement and control over their learning. This encourages all students to stay focused on their learning, which will often give them greater enthusiasm for their studies. Active learning is intellectually stimulating and taking this approach encourages a level of academic discussion with our students that we, as teachers, can also enjoy. Healthy discussion means that students are engaging with us as a partner in their learning.

Students will better be able to revise for examinations in the sense that revision really is 're-vision' of the ideas that they already understand.

Active learning develops students' analytical skills, supporting them to be better problem solvers and more effective in their application of knowledge. They will be prepared to deal with challenging and unexpected situations. As a result, students are more confident in continuing to learn once they have left school and are better equipped for the transition to higher education and the workplace.

What are the challenges of incorporating active learning?

When people start thinking about putting active learning into practice, they often make the mistake of thinking more about the activity they want to design than about the learning. The most important thing is to put the student and the learning at the centre of our planning. A task can be quite simple but still get the student to think critically and independently. Sometimes a complicated task does not actually help to develop the student's thinking or understanding at all. We need to consider carefully what we want our students to learn or understand and then shape the task to activate this learning.

Active learning in Art and Design

Active learning fits well with Art and Design, and there are many opportunities to embed this style of teaching and learning into an Art and Design classroom. Students are often expected to generate their own creative projects and maintain momentum to keep going over a period of weeks or months, but they need to be taught the skills to be able to work in this way. This is usually how students work towards their exam pieces or personal projects for coursework. However, the skills to become an active learner can be embedded into Art and Design learning very early on. Active learning is a working process that can be put in place in the Art and Design classroom and can have positive effects on all areas of study.

Giving and receiving feedback, talking about ideas and presenting to an audience are all valuable transferable skills that Art and Design students learn through this approach. Students are more likely to stay engaged with project work if they have some ownership over the idea. By teaching in this way you are giving your students a toolkit that they can develop to become active learners.

Activities to develop active learning

Here are some examples of activities where you can help students to develop active learning skills:

- writing a project proposal – using a question paper/past paper as a starting point
- identifying an area to start research topics – breaking down topics into subtopics or smaller portions
- talking about Art and Design – evaluating and analysing artworks, exploring a topic to deepen contextual and historical understanding, talking and writing about own work
- ideas generation – problem-solving and creative solutions.

6 Approaches to learning and teaching Art & Design

When introducing a new topic or project, students can often skip ahead to the end result and think too quickly about what their final outcome will be. What you really want is for them to be able to break each stage down and work sequentially through their ideas, letting them make changes as they find out new information. Often students will just get one idea and stick with it, and they can miss opportunities for further exploration around a theme or an approach. Feeling under pressure to create a lot of work quickly can sometimes mean that students produce low-value work, such as biographies of artists, or lots of images from the internet, rather than spending time researching where to start, or analysing their findings and making judgements over how useful or relevant they are. This is where using an active learning approach can help students refocus.

Teacher Tip

Writing a project proposal is something that Art and Design students will be expected to do many times. It's the kind of task that is often set for homework without any proper guidance about where to start or what to include. A good way to prevent students from feeling overwhelmed is to break the task down into sections. It can stop students rushing ahead to what the finished outcome will be, and is a great way to introduce an active learning culture in the classroom.

Instead of launching straight into the finished proposal, students can break the tasks down and focus on them separately, for example, identifying an area to research. A project proposal can help them consider which materials or techniques they think would be most suitable, and that can be where they start their practical investigations.

It's tempting to hand out a really detailed project brief to students that explains exactly what they need to do and by when, but they are more likely to achieve their targets if they feel like they have set them themselves.

> ☑ **LESSON IDEA ONLINE 6.1: ACTIVE RESEARCH: THINK-PAIR-SHARE**
>
> Try this active research task to show your students how they can find out a lot of information in a short time. This project is a think-pair-share teaching method and can be used with students of all ages and abilities.

Project proposal template

When writing a project proposal, keep the final outcome broad so that students don't narrow their ideas before they have started any research. You could just ask them to focus on the first three rows of Table 6.1.

Theme or topic	To design a repeat pattern based on the theme of transport for the seats on a train.
Areas to research	Types of repeat pattern; textile artists who design fabric; types of transport with different seating.
Possible materials	Paint, coloured pencil, fabric paint, heat transfer press, heat transfer dyes.
What the end result might be	A design based on flight as a mode of transport using a calming colour scheme.
How will I review my progress?	Weekly action plan and review, annotation in sketchbook, peer feedback during the project.

Table 6.1: The type of ideas to include on a project proposal.

The next lesson could be based on research activity that uses observational drawing, with students working from a still life to create a large line drawing. The still life could be created from toy trains, cars and planes. From this you could use a viewfinder to select an area of the image as a starting point. Trace this and then flip it to form a mirror repeat.

Figure 6.1: Example of a repeat 'flipped drawing'.

This could then form a design that could be photocopied or traced to explore colour schemes, collage or experimentation with materials. Now that the students have a few possible areas to explore, it will be easier to complete the proposal form. This is the point where students can really engage with their ideas and how to develop them into a personal, creative response. At this point, they are ready to write up the project proposal, identify what they are going to do for the project and set themselves some milestones. Students who still need more support could break this down into a weekly task plan.

Teacher Tip

Introduce a project proposal in the first lesson, but then follow it up by researching the theme, drawing or photographing for research and exploring materials. After a few lessons, ask students to rework their project proposal and see how their ideas have changed and developed. Look at the *Bridges* and *A piece of cake* online assignments: they have been written in this way, as active learning projects.

From this task, the students are learning how to approach a topic, how to explore a theme and how to present their findings. They have also discovered valuable information that will help them meet their aims, such as areas and artists to research, and different types of repeat pattern. They should now be able to identify where they are going to focus their inquiry and break the project down into weekly tasks. When introducing this style of working, students might need templates with a great deal of information such as artists to research, weekly tasks and evaluative language; but you will be giving them a toolkit for this type of learning so that they will be able to work at an independent level in the future.

Creating an atmosphere for active learning

Students can have a great deal of anxiety about making mistakes or the type of work they need to present for assessment. It can feel safer to copy something or work through a piece of work in the same style as an example from the teacher, but this misses opportunities for individuality and creativity. Good technical skills can be developed from referring to examples, but thinking skills need to be learnt in a different way.

In Art and Design it's really important to build an environment where students can make mistakes and learn how to unpick them. If something goes unexpectedly in one direction, they need to be able to retrace their steps and see where things went wrong, or if the result was better than expected they need to understand how it happened. This can help students improve their evaluative skills, so that when talking or writing about their ideas they can move on from descriptive, step by step instructions into ways of describing what impact their research had on the development of their ideas. They can learn how to incorporate feedback into the development of their ideas. Learning to give and receive feedback helps students to trust each other and trust the teacher, and it encourages a healthy learning environment. In Chapter 5 **Interpreting a syllabus** we looked at ways to include peer assessment and self-reflection: these are both active learning tools as they involve the student in their own learning.

Teacher Tip

Active learning is all about engaging students with their own learning so that they feel empowered and realise that learning is a series of discoveries. You can encourage active learning through guided questioning or answer templates; these are especially useful when analysing or comparing Art and Design images. Other ideas include using tasks such as writing case studies or how-to guides, time plans and action plans, and cascade learning and presentations in small groups about a topic that has been researched.

LESSON IDEA 6.2: CASCADE LEARNING

Often, students need some guidance about where to start their research for a new topic. One way to give some structure to the research, while keeping it active, is to set a cascade learning project.

If you have started a new project by producing a mind map, you can ask students to work in small groups of two to three to pick an area to research and then give a short presentation back to the class. This works best when the timescale is really short and the presentations are only around five minutes. It could be about an artist or a technique.

At the end of this activity, everyone in the group will have found out more about a wide range of artists and techniques in a relatively short amount of time.

Ideas at all ability levels

Students can have great ideas even if they don't have the skills to put them into practice. Ideas generation is a skill in itself and you can start this with your youngest students. For less able students, you can still build an active learning classroom, but you might need to offer a smaller range of choices; for example, giving students fewer topics to research or a smaller range of materials and processes to explore while they build their confidence. Building a glossary of new technical vocabulary can help too, and this can include images as well as writing. Recording students talking about their ideas is an excellent way to help them become more confident and better engaged in their own learning.

Barriers to active learning

Active learning sounds like a great idea, but in order to work it needs to have commitment on both sides, from the teacher and from the students. Here are some questions you can consider which will encourage an active learning environment in your classroom:

- Who is directing the learning and generation of ideas?
- Are students involved in selecting topics of interest?
- Are tasks broken down into smaller, more manageable ones?
- Will set work (including homework) be regularly reviewed? Who should do this?
- Is feedback given to students following completion of tasks? Are explanations on how to improve included in this feedback?

How to overcome barriers

Here are some practical tips to help you overcome these barriers and engage students:

- Case study – asking students to write a case study or a how-to guide can make them focus their research on a topic. Find something connected to the theme that they are interested in and ask them to explain it to another student.
- Prompts, question templates, guided research – some students just need a bit more help to get started, so use templates or quizzes to point them in the right direction for their research and development. 'Fill in the blanks' tasks can help students to focus their research around a specific artist or technique.
- Mini projects or skills workshops – these are a great way to break up longer projects. You could focus on a technique or introduce a new material. Give students the time to play and be creative with materials, and explain how they could integrate them into their project.
- Do something different – you can shake up a bored classroom by doing something unexpected. Take them outside to draw, or have a lesson on perspective drawing in a corridor.

> **☑ LESSON IDEA ONLINE 6.3: TEN-MINUTE BOX**
> This lesson idea provides a set of practical tasks that only take ten minutes and can help students to refocus.

What active learning looks like

We've already looked at how writing a project proposal can be a way of introducing active learning for Art and Design students. They can expand on this by using a time plan to cover what they are going to do each lesson. This can be quite simple and is a way to break projects down into stages. Younger students will need guidance with this, but as your students get used to working in this way, they should be able to manage their time more effectively in and out of the classroom.

Problem-solving tasks are full of opportunities for class engagement. Use open project briefs where there is a stimulus and a context, but students have a choice over what they produce. Short projects and design challenges encourage students to have lots of ideas quickly, and can be more active than following a teacher-led demonstration or copying example work.

These activities all give opportunities for a high level of student engagement:

- **Ten-minute box** (Lesson idea 6.3)
- **Using surveys** to give and receive feedback (Lesson idea 5.2)
- **Daily/weekly theme** – this could be a class photography challenge with a different topic each week
- **Think-pair-share** – this could be about an image, an idea, or a technique. (Lesson idea 6.1 can be used or adapted for this)
- **Peer teaching and cascade learning** – after finding out about a technique or artist, students give a presentation or are interviewed by a class partner (Lesson idea 6.2).

Teacher Tip

Encourage problem-solving skills by setting projects with a clear starting point or design challenge, rather than an expected outcome. A quick homework task could be to find an image or story from a newspaper to use as a starting point for a piece of creative work.

How do you measure success?

In an active learning classroom, your students will be able to talk confidently about their ideas, the research areas they want to explore and the challenges they overcame in their work. They will be able to apply a learning process to new tasks, so they can break down a new project into workable stages and identify where to start a project without deciding at the beginning what the end result will be.

Students that can learn in this style will be able to apply this cognitive process to their learning in other subjects.

Summary

Instead of telling your students exactly what they have to do, active learning is about giving them the framework and letting them become involved in their own learning. This creates cognitive pathways and deepens learning. You can build an active learning environment by:

- involving students in writing and updating project proposals

- including time for self-reflection

- adding opportunities to use peer assessment

- breaking long projects down into smaller portions

- using self-reflection in your own teaching and trying something different if students are losing focus.

7 Assessment for Learning

What is Assessment for Learning?

Assessment for Learning (AfL) is a teaching approach that generates feedback that can be used to improve students' performance. Students become more involved in the learning process and, from this, gain confidence in what they are expected to learn and to what standard. We as teachers gain insights into a student's level of understanding of a particular concept or topic, which helps to inform how we support their progression.

We need to understand the meaning and method of giving purposeful feedback to optimise learning. Feedback can be informal, such as oral comments to help students think through problems, or formal, such as the use of rubrics to help clarify and scaffold learning and assessment objectives.

Why use Assessment for Learning?

By following well-designed approaches to AfL, we can understand better how our students are learning and use this to plan what we will do next with a class or individual students (see Figure 7.1). We can help our students to see what they are aiming for and to understand what they need to do to get there. AfL makes learning visible; it helps students understand more accurately the nature of the material they are learning and themselves as learners. The quality of interactions and feedback between students and teachers becomes critical to the learning process.

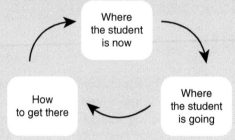

Figure 7.1: How can we use this plan to help our students?

We can use AfL to help our students focus on specific elements of their learning and to take greater responsibility for how they might move forward. AfL creates a valuable connection between assessment and learning activities, as the clarification of objectives will have a direct impact on how we devise teaching and learning strategies. AfL techniques can support students in becoming more confident in what they are learning, reflective in how they are learning, more likely to try out new approaches, and more engaged in what they are being asked to learn.

What are the challenges of incorporating AfL?

The use of AfL does not mean that we need to test students more frequently. It would be easy to just increase the amount of summative assessment and use this formatively as a regular method of helping us decide what to do next in our teaching. We can judge how much learning has taken place through ways other than testing, including, above all, communicating with our students in a variety of ways and getting to know them better as individuals.

What does AfL look like in Art and Design?

In this context we are using Assessment for Learning (AfL) to mean different approaches to formative assessment and giving feedback that can help a student feel engaged in their own learning and improvement. There can be different interpretations of AfL, so before you introduce an approach in your classroom, it would be useful to understand your colleagues' interpretations and whether there is a school policy on AfL.

Students will benefit from understanding what is meant by AfL and when it is going to happen. They should understand the different stages of assessment and feel involved in them, rather than just handing their work in to be marked. In order for it to be effective, the student should play an active part in the process, but this is something they have to learn to do with careful guidance. AfL could be introduced through interim assessments, peer and self-assessments, or critiques and feedback after presentations. You might also teach in a more tutorial style, where students are each given one-to-one attention during their project work as you circulate around the room during lessons.

Teacher Tip

Capturing what you and the student have discussed, and making it accessible, is a key part of AfL. It could be recorded in a journal, reflective log, a home sketchbook, e-portfolio, or on feedback sheets in a folder. Carbon sheets are a quick way of being able to make a copy for yourself and a copy for the student. The important thing is that the student can see what you've both said and agreed.

Using feedback and feed forward

I recently heard the term 'feed forward' instead of feedback, and it was explained as the process of giving feedback that can be used to improve the next process or stage. It's a shift towards target setting and away from an approach that could be negative, especially for weaker students where the focus might be on what they didn't do. I like the idea that it's forward-facing and active, rather than something in the past tense. Feedback at the end of a project often just gets put away with the work and never looked at again. AfL should include active ways of giving feedback that can be used in the future development of work, with strategies for the student to include straightaway to improve their own performance. This is where feed forward comes in: giving constructive guidance to students that recognises what they have accomplished, giving them specific advice about how to improve, and setting action points for the next stage to be achieved. These action points should be linked to the assessment objectives and should build skills over time.

Teacher Tip

An area where students often struggle is in showing how research has influenced their developing ideas. A feed forward action point might be: *'You've explored a range of different artists who use bridges in their work and gathered some striking images from your internet research. Now think about what made you choose those artists and images, e.g. contrast, composition, imagery, tone, and write notes in your sketchbook. Take four to six photos of bridges in the style of the artists or images you liked the most before the end of next lesson.'*

Breaking tasks down into smaller achievable portions can help students manage their time better. It can be easy to praise students for the wrong things by saying things like 'you've made a good start' or 'you tried really hard', but actually these devalue the qualitative language of the assessments and make it sound like students can be rewarded for effort. Praise is a useful motivational tool, but it needs to be used in the right context. A feed forward praise statement could be: 'Your ideas show a clear development and that you've really thought carefully about your research. Choose one or two ideas to develop further, using some of the techniques you explored in the last project and want to try again.'

☑ **LESSON IDEA ONLINE 7.1: TRAFFIC LIGHTS**
This activity aims to help students learn how to give and receive feedback, by using badges or traffic lights.

The key to introducing a new method is to be consistent and give clear expectations to your students about what is happening, and why. It might seem like a lot of work in the first few attempts, but in the longer-term using AfL in your classroom should save you time as students learn to monitor and evaluate their own performance. Students need time to think about what is being said, so if you ask a question, give them space to answer without pre-empting what you want them to say. Reflect on what you have both said, so that the feed forward and AfL comments form part of an ongoing dialogue as the work develops.

Starting AfL

It starts much earlier than you think—you can introduce AfL activities with your youngest students by using target setting to help them achieve short- and long-term goals. The language that you use may also be new to the students, especially if you are teaching in English and this is a second language; your younger students may not yet have the vocabulary to fully understand the differences between levels in the assessment criteria, or the technical language for the processes they are using. By introducing an AfL culture you are also developing critical thinking skills in your students. They will start to understand the connections between ideas and make new ones, and learn how to work in a systematic way to develop ideas and solve problems. For Art and Design, the problems to be solved can be design scenarios or judgement tasks, for example 'I wonder what happens when I mix this material with that one?' As students develop their critical thinking skills they should be able to demonstrate the judgements they have made about elements that are successful and why.

⧉ LESSON IDEA ONLINE 7.2: INTERVIEWING OLDER STUDENTS

This lesson focuses on younger students interviewing older students, and looks at ways to combine interviewing and questioning skills with target setting and receiving feedback.

Teacher Tip

Look back at the self-reflection Lesson idea 5.4 to see where you could incorporate better AfL comments and action points with your students. Asking them to fill in the template can give you something to start the conversation, and make them feel that they are playing an active part in their own formative assessment.

Creating a safe environment for feedback

Students should feel comfortable about making mistakes and learning from them. They should feel able to express what they did and why, and how they feel about their work. For Art and Design, mistakes are a crucial part of the process. Often, when things go in an unexpected direction, a new idea or way of working is found. There's a lot of technical understanding and new materials and processes to learn in Art and Design – these need to be practised over time for skills to develop. Your classroom should have an atmosphere of trust and respect, removing the pressure of getting it right first time, and valuing an iterative process of development and refinement.

Your questioning skills are vital to the success of opening up a dialogue with your students about what they feel went well and what they need to focus on. Open questions prompt longer responses from students than closed questions, which only lead to yes/no answers. Successful questioning uses a mixture of both, as often just using open questions can mean that there isn't a clear enough framework for the students to really understand what it is you are asking them. You can start by asking students which area of their work they feel is most successful, or which idea they think is the best, and then asking them to explain why.

Understanding assessment language

Assessment objectives and criteria are very rarely written directly for the students, as they are developed for teachers and often use quite formal language. They should be shared with students and explained, so that the students feel some ownership over what they are going to be marked against. Understanding the assessment objectives and learning to use this type of language can help students feel engaged and motivated.

Not every piece of work needs to be graded: it's important to add context and explain that at the end of the course, these are the criteria by which the student will be assessed. It also helps if you can show examples of work at a range of grades: this can be from your own school using the work of previous years, or using the Example Candidate Response booklets for each course.

Teacher Tip

Over-assessing can be damaging, as it waters down the expectations of how much work needs to be produced and sets students up to focus on grades. What we really want them to focus on is using strategies that will help them improve and manage their own performance. We want them to learn how to learn. Use AfL as target setting, and encourage students to understand what they need to do and how to manage their time to meet their goals.

Using reflection for self-assessment:

- should make the student feel engaged with their own progress and how to manage their performance
- gives opportunities for using correct technical and specialist vocabulary
- can include valuable feedback from user testing and surveys, or from peer reviews.

Peer assessment and feedback can be very effective and save you time in the classroom.

The difference between reflection and description

This is a critical point. It can make the difference between accessing a higher level in a mark scheme, or being able to make a successful transition from IGCSE level understanding to AS & A Level. Annotation in sketchbooks is often where the reflective and evaluative comments can be located. Students who can only write descriptions of what has happened, and focus on processes, often miss opportunities to deepen their learning by making their comments more reflective. Even simple things like explaining how ideas changed, or what was tried out, can move annotation into a more evaluative and valuable activity.

Often, it's not just the student's technical competence and ability to work individually that differentiates higher level skills; the level of critical understanding and self-reflection is a key indicator. Chapter 8 **Metacognition** explores ways of developing reflective skills and learning how to learn. This really works in harmony with AfL: students need to understand what they have to do and why it's important. This way they become much more engaged with their own progress.

> **☑ LESSON IDEA ONLINE 7.3: FILLING IN THE BLANKS**
> This is a vocabulary builder suitable for a range of abilities. Fill in the blanks, identifying which statements are descriptive and which are evaluative.

Teacher Tip

Surveys are a great way to get feedback quickly, but what the student does with the feedback is important. Do they just ignore it, stick it in their sketchbook, or make adjustments to their idea and move on? What if the feedback was negative? How can you support them to move on from this and turn it into a pivotal point in their ideas development? Showing where things went wrong and were recovered demonstrates critical and contextual understanding.

LESSON IDEA 7.4: FEED FORWARD FLASHCARDS

Think about making some feed forward flashcards or prompts that help students start a dialogue about their work so far. They could be simple laminated cards that students can use on their own or with each other. This might be useful where feedback isn't face-to-face and doesn't include the teacher. Use open questions to start a conversation, such as, 'Which process did you enjoy the most?' Use positive feedback to frame questions, for example, 'The composition makes the image inviting to look at; what materials will you use next?' These types of activity can help build critical evaluation skills, language, vocabulary, and confidence in discussing progress and developing ideas.

Consider other ways of capturing feedback and AfL, such as recording, interviewing, group presentations, or using technology such as e-portfolios. Peer assessment and peer review activities could include tick sheets, interviews, critiques and target setting.

Summary

- Use feedback as a way of assessment for learning (AfL).

- Give students time to think and give meaningful answers.

- Share the work – use peer assessment and reviews.

- Involve the student by asking open questions, such as, 'Which idea do you think is the most successful?'

8 Metacognition

What is metacognition?

Metacognition describes the processes involved when students plan, monitor, evaluate and make changes to their own learning behaviours. These processes help students to think about their own learning more explicitly and ensure that they are able to meet a learning goal that they have identified themselves or that we, as teachers, have set.

Metacognitive learners recognise what they find easy or difficult. They understand the demands of a particular learning task and are able to identify different approaches they could use to tackle a problem. Metacognitive learners are also able to make adjustments to their learning as they monitor their progress towards a particular learning goal.

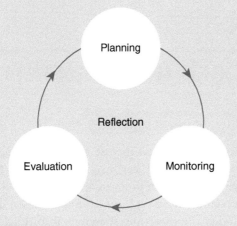

Figure 8.1: A helpful way to think about the phases involved in metacognition.

During the *planning* phase, students think about the explicit learning goal we have set and what we are asking them to do. As teachers, we need to make clear to students what success looks like in any given task before they embark on it. Students build on their prior knowledge, reflect on strategies they have used before and consider how they will approach the new task.

As students put their plan into action, they are constantly *monitoring* the progress they are making towards their learning goal. If the strategies they had decided to use are not working, they may decide to try something different.

Once they have completed the task, students determine how successful the strategy they used was in helping them to achieve their learning goal. During this *evaluation* phase, students think about what went well and what didn't go as well to help them decide what they could do differently next time. They may also think about what other types of problems they could solve using the same strategy.

Reflection is a fundamental part of the plan–monitor–evaluate process and there are various ways in which we can support our students to reflect on their learning process. In order to apply a metacognitive approach, students need access to a set of strategies that they can use and a classroom environment that encourages them to explore and develop their metacognitive skills.

Why teach metacognitive skills?

Research evidence suggests that the use of metacognitive skills plays an important role in successful learning. Metacognitive practices help students to monitor their own progress and take control of their learning. Metacognitive learners think about and learn from their mistakes and modify their learning strategies accordingly. Students who use metacognitive techniques find it improves their academic achievement across subjects, as it helps them transfer what they have learnt from one context to another context, or from a previous task to a new task.

What are the challenges of developing students' metacognitive skills?

For metacognition to be commonplace in the classroom, we need to encourage students to take time to think about and learn from their mistakes. Many students are afraid to make mistakes, meaning that they are less likely to take risks, explore new ways of thinking or tackle unfamiliar problems. We as teachers are instrumental in shaping the culture of learning in a classroom. For metacognitive practices to thrive, students need to feel confident enough to make mistakes, to discuss their mistakes and ultimately to view them as valuable, and often necessary, learning opportunities.

Opportunities for metacognition in Art and Design

Making sure that you embed metacognition into teaching and learning at an early stage can give students the skills to regularly monitor and evaluate their decisions as they research and develop their ideas. This grows into higher order thinking skills, which we would consider to be evidence of critical thinking.

Teacher Tip

Working in a metacognitive style involves students making an active choice about how they are going to learn and why they are choosing one activity over another. In Art and Design, it can be a great way to introduce new vocabulary and verbalise the process that the students are learning. When I'm teaching a new practical task, I break it down into stages and explain each one – a bit like the steps of a dance. Then I show the whole process with all the steps in sequence. I encourage students to photograph or record the process, and annotate these steps later to remind them what they learnt.

For younger students, this can be demonstrated by them describing what they are going to do and why.

Older students can demonstrate this skill by using their experience to decide which materials and process to use, visually and verbally demonstrating their thought processes through notes and drawings in sketchbooks, or when they write out a project plan.

Developing a growth mindset

For younger students, you can introduce metacognition as a 'growth mindset'. They might be interested in the idea of 'thinking about thinking' and taking a more active part in their own learning. It's about making them aware of the thought processes they are using and the decision-making skills they use, rather than waiting to be told what to do by the teacher. Just because we tell them something, it doesn't mean that they have learnt it; they need to make the decision to learn.

For students learning in this environment, it's about knowing what it is they are going to learn, how and why, and how they will know when they've learnt it. These are the questions to ask yourself when planning your teaching and which delivery method to use. Metacognition should be embedded into your delivery and not a separate activity – you can view it as a way of scaffolding other learning activities. This approach links well to the strategies looked at for self-reflection and using peer review to make a really effective learning strategy in your Art and Design classroom.

In other chapters, we explore teaching and learning activities that support a metacognitive approach:

- Feedback and feed forward – using reflection and feed forward to improve students' own learning (see Lesson ideas 5.4 and 7.4).
- Annotation – using evaluative language instead of descriptive, explaining why a material or process was chosen and what the overall effect was (see Lesson idea 7.3 which explores the difference between descriptive and evaluative language).
- Problem-solving – using design briefs to set a design challenge; for example, design the fabric for the seats on a train (see Chapter 3 **The nature of the subject** *Bridges* and Chapter 5 **Interpreting a syllabus** *A piece of cake,* online assignments).
- Developing a set of skills that can be applied to other projects/other learning – these include research, ideas generation, presentation and peer review. (This is covered at several points, but Lesson idea 11.1 provides a worksheet for reviewing digital presentations, which can be used in a range of subjects and not just art).
- Recognising success – using examples to demonstrate good practice at a range of ability levels (see Chapter 11 **Teaching with digital technologies** and consider making a photographic archive of examples of students work, or your own video tutorials to share with students).
- Placing a high value on the learning, not the outcome (see Lesson idea 5.3 which looks at ways of embedding the assessment criteria into learning).

Embedding metacognition techniques into all levels of teaching can improve outcomes for every student, not just for the higher achievers. Working in a way that engages students in their own learning, and therefore in their own performances, helps them understand that learning isn't passive and that it doesn't just *happen* to them. Students really need to be proactive and play a part in learning, finding new information and ways of retaining information. Using metacognition and reflection to help students improve their own performance makes them feel involved and responsible. It can also be a really positive behaviour management tool, especially if you have able but disruptive students who get bored easily and therefore don't always maximise their potential.

Teacher Tip

An easy way to encourage students to engage is to give them a range of choices (even if the choices are quite limited). This will help them to feel that they can give an individual response, or take their own approach, instead of everyone doing the same task.

Teaching practical or technical skills in a metacognitive style

Metacognition sounds great for theoretical or thought-based learning, such as problem-solving, analysing research and planning, but what does it look like for a practical task? Describing what they are doing and why, while demonstrating a practical task, helps students to understand how each stage is related to the next one.

You can break the process down into chunks, demonstrate once or twice, and then ask the students to go through the process themselves. At this point, it's tempting to just keep showing them what they need to do, but that way you can end up doing it all yourself, and then students don't really learn the task.

Instead, you can use questioning skills, such as, 'Do you remember what to do next?' If this only gets you a yes/no response, you can ask, 'What are you going to do next?' or in pairs ask one student to describe the next stage and the other to explain why their description is correct.

For this approach to be successful, aim to use positive reinforcement and conditioning. So if a student gets it wrong, just explain the right way and move on. Depersonalise it, so instead of saying, 'You should have ... ', you can say, for example, 'That happens if there's too much ink on the roller ... '. Add praise when they get it right, but explain why, or what made the difference. This way you are using conditioning and positive reinforcement to embed the best way of doing a practical task. Often there's more than one right way to do something. There's a lot to be learnt from mistakes, which can give you an opportunity to explain the cause and effect, and this contextualises the right way of doing the task. You can learn more from trying to get something right, rather than from getting it right the first time.

Teacher Tip

I always ask students to explain what made the difference when they get it right. Verbalising makes them really think about what they did differently. It's much more effective than me just telling them the right way to do it, and has a 'cascade effect' on the other students who are listening and watching.

Planning, monitoring and evaluating

In many cases, the assessment objectives for art are really the stages of metacognitive thinking (planning, monitoring and evaluating). In a practical subject, these often refer to the development of an idea towards a resolved outcome, and in metacognitive terms they apply to the students' own thinking. These stages should be seen as a loop that feeds into itself, so that evaluating and monitoring are a constant cycle, and planning is ongoing and not just a starting point.

Approaches to learning and teaching Art & Design

A lot of the skills we have covered in this chapter are easy to demonstrate verbally or in writing, but we can also explore what they look like in Art and Design without lots of annotation. Visual examples in sketchbooks or design sheets can be screen grabs showing which filters have been applied, or circles highlighting which pictures were chosen and which ideas were selected to develop further. Drawing pictures or diagrams to explain an idea, and taking photos or drawings that show step by step instructions, are great ways of demonstrating learning. Practising new skills or techniques is an important part of learning. So, if a student can explain why something didn't work and was discarded, it shows that they were really thinking about what they were doing. This can also be seen when a student gives examples of why their ideas didn't work, or they show where they chose the wrong material but then tried again with something different. Evidence of trying and then testing out other materials shows that students are developing and refining by using monitoring and self-evaluation, and that they are looking for the right technique and material to create their chosen outcome.

Figure 8.2: Printmaking tools and materials – students should be able to select the right materials or processes to use for their developing ideas.

Peer teaching

A highly effective way to reinforce new learning is by showing someone else something you have just learnt. This could be a project on its own, or to break up a longer project. It could be a task such as researching an artist who uses an interesting technique or material, then doing a short tutorial to a classmate, working in pairs so that each student learns something new. Part of the task can be to consider how this is metacognition: thinking about what you want the person to learn and choosing the best strategy.

☑ **LESSON IDEA ONLINE 8.1: PEER LEARNING AND METACOGNITION**
This four-week project gives students the opportunity to think about thinking (metacognition). They carry out detailed preparation to teach a skill to another person, then demonstrate the skill and observe peers.

Teacher Tip

Asking students to work in pairs can be something they look forward to, and it can also be beneficial for teachers to work together as mentors. It can really help if you have someone to bounce ideas off, or to encourage you to try things and talk them through together afterwards. This helps you have a metacognitive approach to your own practice and ongoing professional development.

Quick wins and marginal gains

There are some simple, practical things that students can do that have an almost instant impact on the quality of their work. I like to call these quick wins. They often just take a few minutes, but have a positive effect, and show that the students feel proud of and engaged with their work.

Some examples of quick wins:

- For students with untidy handwriting, or who lack confidence with writing or spelling, encouraging them to type out evaluative comments, and cut them out neatly using a ruler, can improve the appearance of their work.
- Writing comments on small card tags that hang in sketchbook pages or in special pockets can add interest to a page of ideas and doesn't take too much time.
- When students feel comfortable and confident in their work, they draw or write straight onto the page, rather than working on sheets and mounting the cut-outs on black sugar paper. Even if they have less ability at drawing, this should be encouraged.
- If your students do want to cut things out of their sketchbook, or use sheets to mount work for a display or supporting studies, a quick win can be planning the layout before sticking it all down. This can make a page of ideas appear visually interesting and sequential.
- Using different scales of images and different textures adds value to a page. Drawing onto photocopies or photos, and working on different types of paper, also show that the students are engaged, have planned ahead and have thought about the best way to articulate their ideas visually.

Marginal gains are those changes that have a positive impact, but over a longer period of time. These tend to be the things that you need to reinforce and remind students to do, such as:

- taking the time to write evaluative and reflective comments
- breaking projects down into stages
- planning ahead.

Even if it feels like this slows a project down at first, it really teaches students how to tackle longer projects.

This is where your use of conditioning and positive reinforcement is important, and shows students that you place a high value on the learning and not just on the outcome. Finding out what students like or enjoy about your lessons can help you find ways to engage them. They might be highly motivated by praise, or enjoy having a choice about their own work, rather than learning by copying or in a house style. This student-led approach takes time to understand, but can lead to better results in the longer term, as students feel more engaged and take responsibility for their learning. This often has a positive impact on attendance and behaviour, which in turn can improve results.

Consider what strategies or actions are appropriate at each stage

Students who are applying a metacognitive approach will be able to ask themselves these questions:

- What should I do to improve my work now?
- What would I do differently next time?
- Can I apply any of this to other tasks/subjects/activities?

We've explored activities where the student has a high level of input over their own idea or is managing a project, and how they can engage in learning a practical task or skill, but we should also consider the value of learning by example. In Art and Design, working in the style of a reference artist is valuable, especially where a new technique, style or material is being introduced. Direct copying should be discouraged, but analysing, contextualising and discovering are highly valuable ways of learning, as are using visual examples of artworks and breaking them down into stages. For example, exploring what works and using formal elements such as composition, scale, texture; considering what message the artist is trying to communicate and how they have done this; describing brushstrokes, materials and colour; and exploring and understanding the use of symbolism and visual language.

These processes all give opportunities for students to see that the artist made choices about what they wanted to communicate, and what the best material, technique or process was to do this. This should help students to see that the approach they are taking to their own learning is appropriate and relevant.

Teacher Tip

There are some ways that you can make your feedback more metacognitive by breaking it down into short active tasks that keep students on track. Think about what kind of feedback you would give to students in the following situations:

- They've done lots of internet research of images or biographical details about an artist, but haven't given any analysis.

- They've taken lots of photos for research, but there's no narrative or cohesion to their recording to show why they chose those photos.

- They've produced a series of unrelated paintings, though each one shows considerable skill.

Summary

- When you are planning your lessons, take the time to consider these questions:

  - What do you want your students to learn?

  - How do you want them to learn it?

  - How will they know when they've learnt it?

- Remember, students learn in different ways and at different paces, so present the information in a range of ways – verbal, visual, written – and allow students to demonstrate that they've learnt it in a range of ways too.

- Give opportunities for quick wins to help students take control of their own learning.

- Include long-term learning and small improvements over time that make a positive difference.

Language awareness

9

What is language awareness?

For many students, English is an additional language. It might be their second or perhaps their third language. Depending on the school context, students might be learning all or just some of their subjects through English.

For all students, regardless of whether they are learning through their first language or an additional language, language is a vehicle for learning. It is through language that students access the learning intentions of the lesson and communicate their ideas. It is our responsibility as teachers to ensure that language doesn't present a barrier to learning.

One way to achieve this is to support our colleagues in becoming more language-aware. Language awareness is sensitivity to, and an understanding of, the language demands of our subject and the role these demands play in learning. A language-aware teacher plans strategies and scaffolds the appropriate support to help students overcome these language demands.

Why is it important for teachers of other subjects to be language-aware?

Many teachers are surprised when they receive a piece of written work that suggests a student who has no difficulties in everyday communication has had problems understanding the lesson. Issues arise when teachers assume that students who have attained a high degree of fluency and accuracy in everyday social English therefore have a corresponding level of academic language proficiency. Whether English is a student's first language or an additional language, students need time and the appropriate support to become proficient in academic language. This is the language that they are mostly exposed to in school and will be required to reproduce themselves. It will also scaffold their ability to access higher order thinking skills and improve levels of attainment.

What are the challenges of language awareness?

Many teachers of non-language subjects worry that there is no time to factor language support into their lessons, or that language is something they know little about. Some teachers may think that language support is not their role. However, we need to work with these teachers to create inclusive classrooms where all students can access the curriculum and where barriers to learning are reduced as much as possible. An increased awareness of the language needs of students aims to reduce any obstacles that learning through an additional language might present.

This doesn't mean that all teachers need to know the names of grammatical structures or need to be able to use the appropriate linguistic labels. What it does mean is that we all need to understand the challenges our students face, including their language level, and plan some strategies to help them overcome these challenges. These strategies do not need to take a lot of additional time and should eventually become integral to our process of planning, teaching and reflecting on our practice. We may need to support other teachers so that they are clear about the vocabulary and language that is specific to their subject, and how to teach, reinforce and develop it.

Building confidence with technical and specialist language

For Art and Design students, there will be lots of new specialist and technical vocabulary to learn. This is the same for all students, regardless of whether or not they are learning in their first language. They will need to learn all the names for the equipment and materials, and be able to describe the processes and follow instructions, in order to work safely in art studios.

A great deal of Art and Design learning includes talking about Art and Design, describing and comparing artworks, and interpreting images of other artists' work. This can be a very enjoyable and rewarding part of the learning process, but it can also be intimidating to a student who lacks confidence in their language skills, regardless of their first language. Some students who enjoy art choose it because they are naturally introverted – it can be a solitary activity and something they can really engage with outside school, without having to mix with other students. You might also encounter students who find spelling and verbalising their ideas difficult, but can communicate incredibly well visually – these students are likely to need more support with new specialist and technical language, especially when it is not in their first language.

Language abilities and understanding can be dependent on age, and you may find that your students might not have the language skills or confidence at the start of secondary education to match their creative and expressive skills. Your aim could be that before the end of secondary level, language and technical skills are firmly in place for students to be able to express their ideas creatively. Students should be able to use the target language to describe the materials, techniques and processes they used, and to fluently articulate their creative work. It's also really important that they enjoy talking about their ideas. By target language, I am referring to the language being used if the students are not being taught in their first language. This aim suits some of the strategies we've explored for metacognition and active learning, and these opportunities for embedding language into the learning can be lost if the creative activities are limited to drawing from photographs or copying artworks.

Teacher Tip

Chapter 8 **Metacognition** describes how you might talk through a demonstration to explain what each stage includes and how it relates to the next stages. You may well find that you need to give students the same information in a range of different ways; for example, verbal instructions, photographs of stages, lists of names for materials and processes, and written instructions. This is the same approach for students learning in their first language, but you may need to allow more time for the specialist language to become embedded and for students to feel confident in using the right words.

Your students will be learning the language and vocabulary related to the materials, tools and processes being used, as well as learning how to describe the techniques they are using. The learning process involves so much more than just watching and repeating a demonstration: students also need to get to grips with all the explanations of what is being done and why, and how each stage relates to the next one. The properties of the materials need to be described, as well as the aims of the task. Just copying a demonstration doesn't mean that learning is taking place, so include a recap on learning by writing up the techniques and talking about the processes and materials that are being used.

Visual language

Visual language is a whole new language in itself, so your students will also be learning how to describe meaning through composition, colours and textures. They will need to explore ways of expressing meaning through semiotics, which is the study of expressing meaning through signs and symbols.

This creative investigation can be used to introduce formal elements, such as line, tone, form, mass, texture and scale; and through mark making and colour theory. This underpinning exploration can be combined with looking at a broad range of artworks and artists, and trying out some of the techniques they have used to convey meaning in their work. A good way to combine practical work with more academic learning is through analysing artworks and using 'compare and contrast' activities to learn how to interpret a painting or an artwork, then producing a piece of work that employs some of the same techniques.

LESSON IDEA 9.1: USING WORKSHEETS FOR LANGUAGE DEVELOPMENT

Using worksheets that show and describe different artworks can be useful for younger students. They could circle the right word or fill in the blanks as an activity to introduce new language.

Higher level students will be able to analyse and explain more about the work as they get used to this type of activity. Some students may feel more comfortable with the academic side and less so with their practical skills, and they should be encouraged with this type of task. Linking the visual language to the written and spoken language helps to embed the learning.

Teacher Tip

Showcasing your students' artworks around the school demonstrates that you value their talents. Use this opportunity to get students talking about Art and Design by adding captions to the artworks on the walls with open questions, such as, 'What do you think the artist was communicating in this picture?' or 'How many different emotions does this image make you feel?' This can make the students engage more with the images on the wall instead of just walking past them, as well as giving you an opportunity to extend learning outside the classroom.

☑ LESSON IDEA ONLINE 9.2: UNDERSTANDING VISUAL LANGUAGE

This lesson idea gives a template to use for comparing artworks and developing skills for analysing and interpreting them. You can adapt this to use with different ages and ability groups, and for different types of artworks.

Language teachers will focus on vocabulary and ways of communicating in different situations. For Art and Design, you can bring these skills into your teaching by encouraging students to use more formal language and conventions for tasks such as research into different artists and artworks. Sketchbooks and annotations can have more informal ways of describing processes and creative ideas.

Practical activities that can provide opportunities for students to combine language skills with practical skills include:

- describing an artwork to another student, then asking them to try and draw it from the description
- directing a film, animation or photo shoot and using storyboards in the target language
- visualising sayings, or illustrating song lyrics or poems
- using a newspaper article as a starting point for an interpretative fine artwork or graphic design task.

A blended learning approach involves ways of supporting in-class teaching and learning with digital methods. In terms of language awareness and development, this could be supported by online portfolios. Students could upload images of their practical activities in class and write a reflective or evaluative comment to support their task, which is then submitted to the teacher for feedback. (This is covered in more detail in Chapter 11 **Teaching with digital technologies**.) It is a good way of separating out language skills from practical skills, so that they can be developed or assessed. (Lesson idea 7.3 is a writing exercise that helps students to differentiate between descriptive, evaluative and reflective language.)

☑ LESSON IDEA ONLINE 9.3: EXPRESSING VISUAL LANGUAGE

This is a practical lesson about using colour and line to express meaning, while investigating the work of other artists.

Teacher Tip

You might have to employ extra strategies to communicate with a group, to ensure that the students have the maximum opportunity to learn. Don't rely on just explaining tasks or using handouts. Include opportunities to recap and to summarise learning. Check the learning is not just at a superficial level, but that the underpinning language of the methods has been understood to the required level.

Interpretative questions and language on question papers

Interpretative questions are more open-ended and tend to include words with several meanings, or that could be interpreted in a range of ways. For example, 'glasses' could mean eyeglasses or drinking glasses. Both are right: the challenge is for the student to make an interesting composition or interpretation. This is where the assessment objectives need to be fully understood, as the student won't be assessed so much on whether or not they have answered the question, but the extent to which the assessment objectives have been met, and the evidence of their research, planning and development. However, if the students don't properly understand the language used in the question paper, their responses might be limited or superficial. This is something to bear in mind if you are translating the question papers for students.

English often has several words for the same or similar things, and if you are translating a question paper, you may need to be able to translate several meanings. Art lessons may or may not be in English, and time to learn the vocabulary and to practise the written and verbal language skills need to be included. Question papers and assessment objectives often use formal language, which you may need to explain to students. Introducing these early on in the course can improve understanding and build confidence with more formal language.

Teacher Tip

Use past question papers to help generate ideas for projects or coursework, and to familiarise students with the format of papers. Encourage students to underline or highlight words they need help with, and to use a dictionary or thesaurus to explore the different meanings of the words for interpretative questions. Use the glossary builder in Lesson idea 3.2 to explain command words and verbs used for Art and Design.

Improving reflective language skills

One of the key differences between an AS/A Level student and an O Level/ IGCSE student is their level of critical understanding and their ability to be self-reflective. While this can be demonstrated visually, it's also often evident in the way that they are able to discuss their ideas, make judgements about their research, and describe ways in which their research and investigations impacted on the development of their ideas and practical outcomes. In order to develop these skills, you can build projects around problem-based learning, such as project briefs and working within a context. This is the scaffolding of working to a design brief or scenario that will give students a starting point and a framework in which to develop their ideas. These projects can provide opportunities to learn specialist technical language and put it into context, so that students learn the application.

Bloom's taxonomy identifies the stages that learners go through to develop higher level thinking skills, as shown in Figure 9.1.

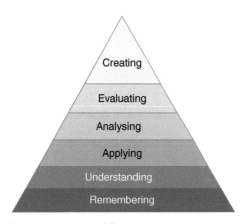

Figure 9.1: Bloom's taxonomy pyramid.

In order for students to be able to make the transition from one level to the next, they need to have spent time over their formative years building up their vocabulary, as well as skills of reflecting and evaluating. We explored ways to be more reflective in Chapter 8 **Metacognition**. Something else to consider when planning courses is how you are going to increase the demand on the language skills of your students as they progress through secondary school.

Teacher Tip

Lesson idea 3.2 talks about ways to start building a glossary – you can extend this over the course to include visual language too.

Collaboration

Taking a collaborative approach to Art and Design and language teaching can provide great opportunities for project work based around a topic, and can provide good opportunities to co-teach with another subject teacher. A combined project could be a mini arts festival, which could have subprojects exploring culture, food and arts on a theme, and creating project work based on this. If you are teaching bilingual students, you may already be using this type of immersive learning, where as much as possible of the curriculum is taught in the target language. In some cases, Art and Design is taught in students' first language, but this can miss opportunities for them to apply the language and engage with the language of the assessment criteria and objectives. Working collaboratively breaks down the notion of separate lessons for different subjects, and can open up a way of teaching Art and Design to bilingual students in a really immersive and creative way.

Teacher Tip

Look for opportunities to make projects more dynamic by working collaboratively with another teacher or subject. Lesson idea 12.1: Trashion/fashion show could be adapted

---

as a creative project brief with another subject, for example Geography, to create garments for a fashion show based on an environmental issue.

Summary

- Consider the different demands of the language for the age group you are working with.

- Think about the hierarchy of the types of language required (Bloom's taxonomy), and ways to build up skills and confidence with reflective language and writing longer amounts of text.

- Blended learning activities combine a range of different teaching and learning activities supported by digital learning. Include opportunities to mix practical and academic tasks to embed language skills in an applied way.

- Collaborative teaching works really well for project work based around a topic, and can be especially effective for younger students.

- Include time for recapping and summarising learning, with a focus on language and specialist vocabulary.

10 | Inclusive education

What is inclusive education?

Individual differences among students will always exist; our challenge as teachers is to see these not as problems to be fixed but as opportunities to enrich and make learning accessible for all. Inclusion is an effort to make sure all students receive whatever specially designed instruction and support they need to succeed as learners.

An inclusive teacher welcomes all students and finds ways to accept and accommodate each individual student. An inclusive teacher identifies existing barriers that limit access to learning, then finds solutions and strategies to remove or reduce those barriers. Some barriers to inclusion are visible; others are hidden or difficult to recognise.

Barriers to inclusion might be the lack of educational resources available for teachers or an inflexible curriculum that does not take into account the learning differences that exist among all learners, across all ages. We also need to encourage students to understand each others' barriers, or this itself may become a barrier to learning.

Students may experience challenges because of any one or a combination of the following:

- behavioural and social skill difficulties
- communication or language disabilities
- concentration difficulties
- conflict in the home or that caused by political situations or national emergency
- executive functions, such as difficulties in understanding, planning and organising
- hearing impairments, acquired congenitally or through illness or injury
- literacy and language difficulties
- numeracy difficulties
- physical or neurological impairments, which may or may not be visible
- visual impairments, ranging from mild to severe.

We should be careful, however, not to label a student and create further barriers in so doing, particularly if we ourselves are not qualified to make a diagnosis. Each student is unique but it is our management of their learning environment that will decide the extent of the barrier and the need for it to be a factor. We need to be aware of a student's readiness to learn and their readiness for school.

Why is inclusive education important?

Teachers need to find ways to welcome all students and organise their teaching so that each student gets a learning experience that makes engagement and success possible. We should create a good match between what we teach and how we teach it, and what the student needs and is capable of. We need not only to ensure access but also make sure each student receives the support and individual attention that result in meaningful learning.

What are the challenges of an inclusive classroom?

Some students may have unexpected barriers. Those who consistently do well in class may not perform in exams, or those who are strong at writing may be weaker when speaking. Those who are considered to be the brightest students may also have barriers to learning. Some students may be working extra hard to compensate for barriers they prefer to keep hidden; some students may suddenly reveal limitations in their ability to learn, using the techniques they have been taught. We need to be aware of all corners of our classroom, be open and put ourselves in our students' shoes.

Differentiation

When we talk about differentiation, we are describing the ways that we can adapt our teaching strategies to the different needs of our students. This is so that each student in the classroom has access to the information they need in order to learn and make progress, and some students may need the same information in a variety of ways. An inclusive classroom methodology can apply to any classroom, and not just to students with special requirements.

In order to make my teaching as accessible as possible to students across a wide ability range, I ensure that I include more time for tasks such as recapping, target setting, and tutorials where we talk through ideas and progress. Often students can be brilliant at creative thinking and talking about ideas but find putting their ideas on paper difficult.

Teacher Tip

Handouts and project notes can be useful. I try to print them on pastel-coloured paper and encourage students to take photos, notes or recordings of important points in the lesson, so they can revisit them later. Some students may have extra support sessions with a teaching support assistant. Making sure that the assistant also has all the project notes, and understands what the tasks involve, will help your students' progress.

Teacher Tip

For students with short attention spans, keep projects short and introductions brief, and have a range of different activities set up around the room so that they can dip in and out of different tasks. For example, if space allows, you could have a printmaking area set up, or a sewing machine. Even a clean table for writing up work or a quiet corner for students to focus and catch up can be useful. Some students might work better if they are allowed to listen to music, or get up and walk around sometimes, as long as they are working well.

The most useful factor for achievement is engagement. The level to which the students are interested and engaged in the activity will play a large role in how much they achieve or make progress. This is where you can use differentiation in planning your teaching and learning activities, so that you can offer a range of opportunities for students to become engaged in their learning. We've explored active learning, and using reflection and peer review as metacognition tools. These are things that you can embed into your teaching to build an inclusive learning environment. When students feel engaged, they feel motivated, behaviour improves and they make progress. Attendance can also improve, and low level disruptions can be quickly addressed and stopped from escalating by using strategies to help students refocus and manage their own learning.

Teacher Tip

Look back over some of the activities in Chapter 6 **Active learning** for keeping students motivated, and try to adapt them for students with additional learning needs. Simple strategies to make your teaching more inclusive include:

- using a clear font and larger type on your project handouts
- making lesson presentations available to students, either through the school's virtual learning environment or their own memory sticks
- giving students templates for time plans and self-reflection.

Teaching methods for an inclusive learning environment

There are several different tools you can use in your teaching to make it more accessible to a broad range of students. This isn't just applicable to students with additional needs, but can be useful for all classes. In some groups, the different requirements of your students can be obvious, but for others they may be hidden. Students can often develop sophisticated ways of dealing with or hiding an issue that they feel sensitive about.

Here are some examples of different teaching methods you could use:

- **Tasks**: different tasks for different ability levels, but available to all; for example, a task sheet that covers basic, intermediate and extension tasks. Set a range of tasks that get progressively more demanding, or require more independent work. Think about setting tasks that require the student to set the level of demand.
- **Group work**: include opportunities for collaborative and group work. 'Buzz groups' (small discussion groups) of two to three students are great for tasks like research, presentations, tutorials, peer review and peer teaching. Including time for these small groups to feed back to the rest of the class can help build trust and confidence about presenting ideas.
- **Information**: use a range of different resources so that the information is available in a variety of different ways; for example, written, visual, verbal, on white board, and on project sheets. Use different coloured papers for everyone, so that students with visual needs or dyslexia don't feel singled out. Keep sentences and instructions short.
- **Pace**: think about the pace of your lessons, how much you need to cover and how long you expect tasks to take. Allow time for recap of instructions and dealing with late or disruptive students, but keep to task and pace. Use verbal summaries of instructions and aims to keep students on task and able to understand why what they are doing is important.
- **Praise**: a lot of disruptive behaviour is because of anxiety. It can be performance anxiety, fear of a lack of knowledge being exposed, fear of failure, or fear of achievement. Some students feel safer being in trouble than being praised. Use praise as a motivator and a reward.
- **Outcome**: it's great if you can have individual responses to a theme, rather than identical outcomes. You can have a small option of outcomes within a range (for example, to design a t-shirt or a bag), so that students feel some ownership and individuality over their outcomes.

Questioning, language and praise

Guided questioning can be a highly effective tool for building an inclusive learning environment and differentiating between the needs of your students. Using open questions to initiate a conversation with your students about their work can help improve their language skills, and can give them the chance to discuss their ideas and progress. Short sentences, clear instructions and appropriate praise should be used. Your skills at asking the right questions are important here, so use a range of open questions to get students to talk about their ideas, such as, 'Which part do you think worked the best?' and 'What else can you do?' The answers can be captured either in written form or recorded, so that it can be counted towards assessments. It is also important to give students enough time to think about their answers, but this may take longer for students with additional needs, so patience is needed. Your listening skills are as important as your questioning skills.

There should be regular progress monitoring and feedback, but it's also important not to over-assess, as this can devalue assessment. Regular reviews and feedback can be used to set targets, and this can be especially useful for students who make slow progress or just need a bit more support and time to explain tasks, or to talk about their ideas. Too much assessment can lead to a culture of grade inflation, as students expect that their grades will go up every time they are marked, when in fact progress isn't always linear. When a range of different skills are being taught and assessed, it's normal to be better at some things than others. Understanding that learning isn't always about getting the right answers can motivate students to do the best they can, so they feel proud of their achievements, whatever level they are at. For some students, just staying at the same level is a huge achievement.

In some cases, students with additional needs may also suffer from a lack of self-belief or low self-esteem. Careful use of praise, and using language that helps to develop a positive mindset, can help students to overcome self-limiting thoughts. Praise as a motivator can be as simple as asking students questions about their work and listening to them talk through their ideas. By agreeing with the choices they have made about their work, you will be giving them validation that their ideas are worth developing. When students feel confident to give and receive peer feedback, it improves their feeling of belonging and self-worth, and this will demonstrate that they are a valued member of the group. This is especially useful for students with low self-esteem or lack of self-belief that could be limiting their creativity or their potential in the classroom.

Teacher Tip

Reframing the negative statements that students often say, such as altering 'I can't do that' to 'I can't do that … yet', can be a simple but effective tool to turn negative mindsets into positive ones. This is also especially useful if your students are being taught in a second language – language issues could be adding to the barriers.

Using a student-centred approach

A student-centred classroom is a safe, inclusive, caring and empowering environment, where students feel their contribution is valuable and they are not afraid of making mistakes. The teacher is a facilitator and role model, who rewards appropriate behaviour as a motivator, rather than punishing negative behaviour.

Students learn how to self-monitor, make changes to their behaviour, and take responsibility for their own learning and progress or lack of progress, too. This doesn't mean a loss of authority or respect in the classroom: moving the teacher away from lecturing at the front of the class can lead to a more inclusive style of teaching in which students are better engaged.

Teacher Tip

In my teaching, I mainly use a student-centred approach. I think about what and how students are going to learn, and make sure that my plans can be adapted to suit their needs. With a student-centred approach, discovering meaning is central; I encourage students to make learning constructs and cognitive links through problem-solving and active learning, and I recognise that reflection is the key for effective learning.

Look at your own teaching plan and highlight the opportunities to make your teaching more student-centred and less teacher-led.

Whole class strategies to improve behaviour

One of the key factors in behaviour management is for the teacher to be consistent. This applies to praise as well as sanctions. In the early part of term, you can work with your students to develop a behavioural contract for classroom conduct. One of my key principles is that I start on time and finish on time. Keeping a good pace is important to me as a teacher, so I work hard to set the appropriate amount of work. I also use extension activities for classes that work quickly; for classes that work slowly the focus can be on quality and finish, rather than quantity produced. Lessons should have a clear start: they don't all have to follow a format (such as using a PowerPoint presentation to introduce a topic), but explaining the expectations of the session is important, as it sets out what is expected of the student.

Using project plans and project booklets that break lessons down into the tasks and topics to be covered can be effective for all types of students. This can help reduce barriers for students with additional needs because everyone can have all the information in one place. Some students may have additional support, and these booklets or project plans can be useful for the support tutor to understand what is expected of a student, or what still needs to be achieved.

Rewards and sanctions should be consistent and on display. Sometimes, positive feedback is enough of a reward. With older students, the reward might be allowing them to listen to music or work in the classroom on their own. Sanctions might be extra tasks or a loss of time on the computers. If you set homework, it's important to review it regularly, and this can be part of the contract that you must keep (see Lesson idea 10.1). For all my classes, I factor time to tidy up into the lesson, so that I'm teaching students to respect their working environment, to look after their tools and equipment, and to manage their time. Consider trying the following:

- Use advance organisers – these are project booklets that set out the expectations and tasks, and show how they all fit together.
- Consider your handouts and project notes and decide whether or not written instructions are the most effective way to frame a particular task. Check that your teaching materials aren't causing barriers to learning for students with additional needs.
- Use a variety of teaching methods to keep things interesting; for example, tutorial teaching, lectures, circulating classroom, small groups, quizzes, games, prizes, a weekly photo challenge. Or, putting work up on the wall and talking about it, taking notes, giving feedback and directions.
- Include opportunities for lots of recap, summary sheets, time planning or advance organising.
- Carry out careful target setting, ensure that interim reviews are linked to the project and feedback is broken down into portions.
- Make sure that the assessment criteria are fully explored during projects, so that students know how they will be assessed and have an opportunity to meet all the criteria.

To build a trusting and caring classroom, you can use frequent small group work with different students, so that everyone knows each other and exclusive groups are discouraged. Build trust between students by setting joint research projects and holding regular informal critiques. Use praise, reward positive behaviour, and encourage students to feel comfortable giving and receiving feedback.

Teacher Tip

Praise should be meaningful and related to the task, but not necessarily just about the quality of the completed outcome. For example, you could point out good practice by saying, 'You have captured lots of ideas well in your mind map', or 'You managed to overcome several challenges with organising the colours for your printmaking and you didn't give up.'

Remember that giving excessive praise to one or two students may create problems in the classroom and put pressure on those students who then feel they have a lot to live up to. Using qualitative words from the assessment criteria should be done with care, so as not to mislead. For example, if you tell all your students their work is 'good', but they don't get a 'good' final mark, it may make them lose faith in your judgement.

☑ LESSON IDEA ONLINE 10.1: CLASS CONTRACTS

This lesson idea asks students to write a class contract. This activity is great for the start of term, or when working with a new group to establish ground rules and codes of conduct.

Summary

- Think about the different needs of your students and how you can adapt your teaching to meet their needs.

- Allow for different routes to the same outcome, rather than one way of doing things.

- Use a variety of teaching methods, and be consistent and appropriate with your rewards and sanctions.

- Reframe negative thought processes and statements into positive declarations, to foster a positive mindset.

- Improvement is not always linear, and for some students maintaining a certain level is as valuable as making progress.

Teaching with digital technologies

11

What are digital technologies?

Digital technologies enable our students to access a wealth of up-to-date digital resources, collaborate locally and globally, curate existing material and create new material. They include electronic devices and tools that manage and manipulate information and data.

Why use digital technologies in the classroom?

When used successfully, digital technologies have the potential to transform teaching and learning. The effective use of technology in the classroom encourages active learning, knowledge construction, inquiry and exploration among students. It should enhance an existing task or provide opportunities to do things that could not be done without it. It can also enhance the role of assessment, providing new ways for students to demonstrate evidence of learning.

New technologies are redefining relationships and enabling new opportunities. But there are also risks, so we should encourage our students to be knowledgeable about and responsible in their use of technology. Integrating technology into our teaching helps prepare students for a future rooted in an increasingly digitised world.

What are the challenges of using digital technologies?

The key to ensuring that technology is used effectively is to remember that it is simply a resource, and not an end in itself. As with the use of all resources, the key is not to start with the resource itself, but to start with what you want the student to learn. We need to think carefully about why and how to use technologies as well as evaluating their efficiency and effectiveness.

If students are asked to use digital technologies as part of their homework, it is important that all students are able to access the relevant technology outside school. A school needs to think about a response to any 'digital divide', because if technology is 'adding value', then all students need to be able to benefit. Some schools choose to make resources available to borrow or use in school, or even loan devices to students.

Safety for students and teachers is a key challenge for schools and it is important to consider issues such as the prevention of cyber-bullying, the hacking of personal information, access to illegal or banned materials and distractions from learning. As technology changes, schools and teachers need to adapt and implement policies and rules.

One of the greatest pitfalls is for a teacher to feel that they are not skilled technologists, and therefore not to try. Creative things can be done with simple technology, and a highly effective teacher who knows very little about technology can often achieve much more than a less effective teacher who is a technology expert. Knowing how to use technology is not the same as knowing how to teach with it.

Digital resources in Art and Design

Digital information has completely changed Art and Design in terms of teaching and as an industry. Students are highly skilled at finding information on the internet, and at taking photos with their phones and sharing them. They really understand how to communicate through images, and using digital technology as a means of recording is second nature.

What they are not so good at is analysing this information and organising it into something useful. Often, they can't tell what information is real and what is misleading or incorrect. Students are able to gather a lot of information quickly, but then they can't always see which elements are the valuable elements. They need guidance on synthesising information and verifying authenticity of their sources.

Students have really embraced social media and photo-sharing platforms, and this ease of capturing, recording and sharing information should be included in your own teaching. Students do need to learn how to use these platforms safely, in terms of sharing information, understanding personal boundaries, respecting copyright and intellectual property, and protecting their own ideas and online identities.

There's definitely a place for having digital devices and access to the internet in the classroom. I see Digital resources as a tools; something to save time and share information. Even simple things such as being able to spellcheck work, or use dictation software, can improve student outcomes. Being able to access information about lessons outside the classroom can mean that students can manage their own learning better, both for students who want to do extra work and get ahead, and for those students who need a bit more support or have help outside lessons.

The digital teacher

Digital tutorials can also be incredibly valuable to you in your classroom – they can support and extend your own teaching by providing access to a wealth of techniques that you might not know or be able to resource yourself. Students are so hungry for information and this is another way of sharing it with them.

Technology that can save teachers time should also be embraced. Schools that really want to improve their digital teaching should allow time and resources for staff development and training.

Teacher Tip

Try recording your own tutorials and demonstrations of practical techniques to support your teaching. Even a short video showing skills and techniques can be really useful for students. This could be made available on an e-learning platform if you have one at your school. Or you could use a private blog or channel on a video-sharing site that students can access. Even showing a video to support a practical demonstration can have a positive effect.

For some students, the opportunities provided by digital resources, such as photo-sharing websites, camera phones and the internet, will bring an extra dimension to an already developed skill set. But for weaker students, there can be an over-reliance on these tools, and a loss of confidence in their own observation and drawing skills. Drawing from a photograph is never as useful as drawing from an object (it creates a very flat image), but using a camera to record lots of views of the same object, or colours and textures for future development work, can be incredibly useful. Using a phone to record feedback or talk about ideas can be invaluable for students who need extra instructions and support, or for those who want to write up their notes neatly at home.

Teacher Tip

Filming yourself teaching can be useful for your own professional development. It can help you to think about your own body language and ways of communicating. It can be informative to see how your students are responding to you at different stages in your teaching. If you do this, you must make sure that your class is aware and that parents have given their consent for their child to be filmed.

> ☑ **LESSON IDEA ONLINE 11.1: WHAT TO LOOK FOR IN DIGITAL PRESENTATIONS**
> In this lesson, students complete a worksheet when they are observing each other's digital presentations, and when planning their own class presentations.

The 24-hour classroom

As an art teacher, I mainly work in studios rather than a traditional classroom, so many of my teaching spaces haven't even got a whiteboard, let alone access to the internet. I relish the opportunities that digital teaching brings to Art and Design teaching. The ability to quickly show a range of different artists' work can have an instant positive impact on a student who is struggling with the direction of their work. I encourage my students to take photos on their phone, where school policy will allow it, as these progress photos can be added to their sketchbooks and development sheets. Photographs of work that have been taken while ideas have developed help to add authenticity to student work, and give students a prompt for talking about how their work developed and changed, or what tools and materials were used.

I use a tablet device in the classroom and I have access to all my teaching notes, handouts and planning. I can take photos of student work to document progress and to act as reminders when I write reports. These photos also form a digital archive of my own marking, which helps me to be more effective and assess accurately year on year. Films of me teaching have been used for teacher training and to show an open classroom approach in my school. Videos recorded on my phone have transformed the way I use digital technologies in my own teaching, as I can use short film clips of practical tasks as a refresher and skill builder for my students, so they can access the information any time from a photo-sharing platform.

Teacher Tip

Set boundaries about when you will respond to questions outside your own lessons. Students will learn how to use digital technology from you, and this includes respecting privacy by not filming or taking photographs without permission, and appropriate use of emails or group chats.

Virtual Learning Environments

Schools that use a Virtual Learning Environment (VLE) are helping
to change the traditional classroom by making teaching and learning
information accessible at all times. Students can access information about
their next lessons, or recap on handouts and key themes from previous
lessons. All the information can be held in one place, and students can
customise it to make it more personalised and catered to their needs.
This type of interaction develops a greater sense of engagement in
students' own learning, and it can save time for teachers because they
can plan ahead and know that the information will be made available to
students in weekly segments. This can be a great time-saver for students
who struggle with time management or organisation.

There are several free, open source options available to schools, and
there are also paid-for services that can be custom-made for schools.
There is a lot of choice for schools who wish to move towards digital
learning. How far each school can become digital will depend on access
to the internet and whether or not the students have access to a phone
or tablet.

Some VLEs have an option for a forum and moderated group chat,
which means that students can pose and answer questions during school
time and out of hours. Many have the function for students to be able
to hand in work for assessment, and there are also packages that can host
learning modules that have been prepared in advance. E-portfolios are
particularly relevant for Art and Design students, as they can complement
traditional sketchbooks by being able to host students' digital photos,
films and animations, alongside scans of sketchbook work, development
work, videos of students talking about their ideas, or films of them. These
e-portfolios can contain links to blogs or relevant websites, and the whole
content can be zipped up as a unique URL and sent off to a potential
employer or university application, as a showcase of the student's work.

Teacher Tip

Asking students to produce a video tutorial is a very effective
way of testing that they have understood a particular topic or
technique, and it can be great fun. These video tutorials can
be used as a teaching resource or a technical archive for other
classes, and reduces the pressure on the teacher to create
all the video tutorial information. (Lesson idea 7.2 is about

interviewing older students; this would be a great activity to be filmed and made available on the VLE.)

Digital parents

A VLE can also be extremely valuable to parents who wish to be more engaged with what their children are learning. There are several software options available that can have a parental login and notifications. They can be useful to reward students for positive achievements, and can also be used to quickly alert parents to behavioural problems or to a student who is at risk of falling behind. This means that the problems can be addressed and resolved quickly. Parental involvement can be an effective tool for helping to improve attendance and achievement through improved home/school communications. Some VLEs have built-in progress reporting, and these can be shared within school and with parents to monitor their child's progress.

Access to digital resources

Many teachers are concerned that their own digital skills may not be up to date, and that the resourcing of equipment and software is not achievable in their school. This is where I would reinforce that digital technology is a tool, to be used or not, as you see fit.

Fairness and access is also something to think about. Not every student is going to be able to provide their own device, so the school needs to discuss and decide whether it is a required piece of equipment, or a desirable extra. There might be situations where students can share, or some may be able to provide their own equipment, and you should consider whether students will be disadvantaged if they don't have access to the equipment. Not all homes have internet access, but increasingly we assume that they do. Digital poverty can be something that families don't feel able to discuss, and schools' requirements for new technology can put extra pressure on already stretched families. This is where it's important to really consider if the use of digital technology is going to improve achievement, reduce barriers and increase engagement. For digital technologies to be essential to improve teaching and learning, they need to be more than just ways of accessing the internet in the classroom and have some sort of efficiency-saving elsewhere, for example, by reducing the need to buy and carry textbooks.

Traditional vs. modern

Think about what process the digital technology is enhancing or replacing. Are you making processes more efficient, or just swapping one problem for another?

Digital technologies in Art and Design can include using computer-aided design to produce digital files for machine cutting, rapid prototyping, 3D printing, digital printing for fabric, laser cutting and water jet cutting for wood, metal and plastics, games design, 3D animation, manipulating images, and using moving image. Digital learning has become completely embedded in the Art and Design industry. However, drawing hasn't been replaced, and the more traditional skills of communicating ideas and observation through drawing are just as valuable as ever.

Teacher Tip

QR (Quick Response) codes are an easy way of making information available to students. It could be something like a glossary, a tutorial, or information about an artist or artwork that students can access quickly, or create and share digitally when they scan the QR code.

The benefits of using technology

Before you commit to digital technologies, think about what benefit they are going to bring to you as a teacher, your learning environment and your students.

VLE	E-portfolio
Information all in one place	Great for uploading images, documents, video and audio
It is useful for the whole school to adopt an online system	Student and teachers can add written or verbal commentary and feedback
Great for planning	Students can show development of ideas over time
Helps students to stay on track and prepare for lessons	Work is less likely to be lost or forgotten

VLE	E-portfolio
Can improve home/school communication	Demonstrates authenticity of students' work and can show the iterative changes as their ideas have been developed
Can promote cost savings from fewer manual processes and reduced printing costs for teaching resources	Can be retained as a showcase of a student's work for their own reference, and for external partners, such as potential employers or university applications
Less effective for submitting work for assessment, but the technology is improving	Can be a useful resource for your own teaching and can be shared within teaching teams
Can be combined with progress and attendance reports for greater monitoring of students' progress	

Table 11.1: Benefits of VLEs and E-portfolios.

Things to consider:

- creating a comprehensive school policy covering safe use, bullying prevention, confidentiality, malpractice and use of student data
- 'future proofing' software and systems – making sure that investment is made in equipment and software that won't date quickly or need a high level of maintenance
- selecting the best fit software and devices
- considering time-saving and related efficiency savings against the up front costs and maintenance costs.

The tablet-friendly classroom

Some schools are moving over to becoming tablet-friendly schools, starting with the junior schools and working their way up. It really demonstrates a culture shift and an embracing of a new way of working. The positive benefits can be as tangible as saving money on textbooks and cutting down on paperwork. Also, students can just bring a tablet learning device instead of books for each subject, so there's less to carry and less to forget. There are several different types of tablets available, and a whole range of educational apps and software. Students will need effective digital skills in order to survive in higher education and employment, and digital literacy can increase student's employability. But there are barriers to overcome in terms of access, fairness and cost. Additionally, most exams are still written by hand, so students still need to be able to write for several hours and these motor skills should be developed alongside digital skills.

Measuring impact

It might be useful to run a trial of using digital technology, then evaluate the impact this has had on students and the pilot groups, before you invest more or widen it out to the whole school. It can also be valuable to keep monitoring the impact. There might be some subjects or groups where digital resources have had a greater impact, and other subjects where traditional methods are working well and the impact is negligible.

Impact might be measured in improved retention of students, reduced absence, greater overall satisfaction, improved results and progress, greater volume of work, and improved quality of work submitted. Or it could be something as simple as being able to share progress with parents. Recognising the achievements of the day and sharing it with parents could have a beneficial impact on a student's achievements and well-being, that in turn could lead to improved performance.

Running a trial first could uncover unexpected benefits, or potential ways to widen opportunities. Embedding digital technologies in your teaching might strengthen student engagement, and it could be an opportunity to review the school values to see if they can be improved by adopting a more digital approach.

Summary

In order for digital teaching to be effective in your school, the following should be discussed and regularly reviewed:

- Have a detailed school policy on what is an acceptable use of digital technology.

- Be clear about how digital technology is being used to improve teaching and learning experiences.

- Consider how the impact of these resources will be measured and reviewed.

- Set aside time for staff development and staff training to engage with digital resources and technology.

- Ensure that access is fair so that all students have equal access to resources that can improve their learning.

12 | Global thinking

What is global thinking?

Global thinking is about learning how to live in a complex world as an active and engaged citizen. It is about considering the bigger picture and appreciating the nature and depth of our shared humanity.

When we encourage global thinking in students we help them recognise, examine and express their own and others' perspectives. We need to scaffold students' thinking to enable them to engage on cognitive, social and emotional levels, and construct their understanding of the world to be able to participate fully in its future.

We as teachers can help students develop routines and habits of mind to enable them to move beyond the familiar, discern that which is of local and global significance, make comparisons, take a cultural perspective and challenge stereotypes. We can encourage them to learn about contexts and traditions, and provide opportunities for them to reflect on their own and others' viewpoints.

Why adopt a global thinking approach?

Global thinking is particularly relevant in an interconnected, digitised world where ideas, opinions and trends are rapidly and relentlessly circulated. Students learn to pause and evaluate. They study why a topic is important on a personal, local and global scale, and they will be motivated to understand the world and their significance in it. Students gain a deeper understanding of why different viewpoints and ideas are held across the world.

Global thinking is something we can nurture both within and across disciplines. We can invite students to learn how to use different lenses from each discipline to see and interpret the world. They also learn how best to apply and communicate key concepts within and across disciplines. We can help our students select the appropriate media and technology to communicate and create their own personal synthesis of the information they have gathered.

Global thinking enables students to become more rounded individuals who perceive themselves as actors in a global context and who value diversity. It encourages them to become more aware, curious and interested in learning about the world and how it works. It helps students to challenge assumptions and stereotypes, to be better informed and more respectful. Global thinking takes the focus beyond exams and grades, or even checklists of skills and attributes. It develops students who are more ready to compete in the global marketplace and more able to participate effectively in an interconnected world.

What are the challenges of incorporating global thinking?

The pressures of an already full curriculum, the need to meet national and local standards, and the demands of exam preparation may make it seem challenging to find time to incorporate global thinking into lessons and programmes of study. A whole-school approach may be required for global thinking to be incorporated in subject plans for teaching and learning.

We need to give all students the opportunity to find their voice and participate actively and confidently, regardless of their background and world experiences, when exploring issues of global significance. We need to design suitable activities that are clear, ongoing and varying. Students need to be able to connect with materials, and extend and challenge their thinking. We also need to devise and use new forms of assessment that incorporate flexible and cooperative thinking.

Art and Design is a global industry

One of the most interesting aspects of teaching and learning Art and Design is finding out about other artists and designers from around the world. You might already feel like your students have a global thinking approach, and this might be something that comes naturally to them. Often, teenage students pick up on global issues for their self-negotiated projects, and they are interested in the world around them and the effect they can have to improve things. Projects that are based around raising awareness or changing perspectives work well for subjects like graphics and animation. Fine art students are often keen to explore more challenging issues, or topics that they feel passionately about. It will be up to you, as the teacher, to manage the direction these projects take and create a balance between a meaningful exploration of topics, as well as being challenging and pushing boundaries.

Drawing inspiration from a wide range of sources is an easy and effective way to have a more global approach to projects. There's so much information available on the internet in terms of Art and Design from around the world that it can make researching easy, but students still need to be taught how to research effectively, and how to make sure their sources are reliable and the information is correct. Accessing journals, magazines, newspapers and books that cover a range of topics can help extend research skills, and also improve awareness of global issues without restricting research to Art and Design. These activities develop students' critical thinking and their contextual analysis skills.

Art and design is an enormous global industry with so much potential for interesting and diverse jobs. In some cases, local creative employment opportunities might be limited and students may have to travel away from home for higher education and employment. Researching these opportunities can help students to become more aspirational about their own career goals and what they need to achieve to maximise their potential. In some places, there may be a diverse arts economy; for example, there might be an active tourist trade and potential for self-employment creating and selling Art and Design products for tourists or export. These opportunities should be reflected in the type of skills development that is covered in the secondary curriculum, so that students are being equipped with the means to sustain a career or to make progress on a career pathway that can lead to employment.

Global issues in Art and Design

In terms of teaching Art and Design and considering global thinking, Table 12.1 lists high priority topics that projects should explore. Note that in this table, by products I mean designed outcomes, such as furniture, packaging, or clothing. Recent high profile issues have included the increase in plastic waste through the use of takeaway coffee cups and plastic straws, neither of which biodegrade or can be recycled.

Issue	Example
Ethics	Making sure that design work is original and not copied. Making sure that ideas improve people's lives and are not designed to cause destruction or harm.
Life cycle	Designing or making products and considering how they are made, used and disposed of.
Manufacturing processes	Designing items whose manufacturing processes are not harmful to the people involved in producing them, or to the environment.
Renewable resources	Exploring ways to use renewable resources and manufacturing processes that don't produce hazardous waste.
Carbon footprint	Ensuring that design and manufacture don't cause hazardous gases, or waste. Looking for opportunities to reduce transporting goods by sea or air, and using local suppliers where possible.
Tourism	Boosting local economy by producing items to sell to tourists that use local skills and materials.

Issue	Example
Economics	Considering the human cost when developing and designing products, and not just looking for the cheapest solution.
Sustainability	Considering ways of making sure that products can be made long-term, while addressing the points above. For example, reducing the need for disposable items that can't be recycled.

Table 12.1: A list of global issues in Art and Design that can be explored further.

Design ethics is one way of introducing global thinking into Art and Design projects. It can be approached at every level, but may have more relevance for older students. Issues such as sustainability and ethics can be discussed and explored in Art and Design. Ethical considerations include:

- Creating Art and Design products that improve people's lives and don't lead to harm in any way, either through their manufacture, use or end of life
- Copying is a huge issue in Art and Design, and students must learn to protect their ideas.
- Accessibility – creating affordable rather than prohibitively expensive items, thinking about cost and profit, encouraging access to well-designed products that make life easier for the user, or to digital technology that simplifies tasks.

Fashion design and manufacture is a good starting point for exploring global issues in a way that students can relate to, as it is possible to find out about companies with an ethical policy. This can be ethical in terms of how they source their raw materials, and also in terms of how employees are treated in the construction of garments.

Keeping on the fashion design theme, recycling clothes is a way of introducing sustainability as a topic in Art and Design, and challenging ideas of consumerism and the end of life of mass-produced products. Topics around sustainability can include looking at the way minerals and raw materials are mined and transported for manufacture, and the end of life for designed products. This could be researching packaging, manufacture, life span and what happens to the items after they are used. For example, can the items be recycled, do they decompose without causing environmental damage, and are they safe to use at all stages of their lifespan?

Figure 12.1: Recycled clothes.

☑ LESSON IDEA ONLINE 12.1: TRASHION/FASHION SHOW

This lesson idea is aimed at producing new garments and accessories from recycled garments or products. In order to be more accessible to all students, the lesson can be combined with an alternative brief of designing packaging or a display product from a waste product; for example, coffee machine pods, recycled packaging, or repurposed building materials.

The balance between tourism and economics are important topics for art students in terms of designing and making products to sell. There will be some cases where students develop an interest in making and producing crafts as a way of life, which can be sold to tourists or exported, and can become commercially successful. A skilled workforce can contribute to the economic success of a country. If you have a particular local craft or custom that is highly regarded, it should be included in the curriculum. It might be batik, ceramics, metal work or weaving, and the value of these crafts and the skills associated with them should be taught as part of an Art and Design programme, so that they are not lost over time.

Digital entertainment is a growing industry, and digital skills such as games design, music, film and TV have their roots in an inclusive and broad arts education, where students have access to a variety of art forms, and are encouraged to develop their skills and creative voice.

Teacher Tip

Find out what global issues affect your students and see if you can harness their interest and passion into a self-negotiated active learning project. This could work as a great starter project for a think-pair-share project, where students research a topic and present their findings back to the class. A good place to start could be by reading newspaper reports and looking for local environmental campaigns, or international issues such as deforestation, poverty, travel, renewable resources or pollution. This could be set as an active learning project or a self-negotiated coursework project for older students.

Collaboration

Developments in communication technology have made collaboration easier between companies and partners located in different places. For Art and Design, this can mean outsourcing aspects of design, manufacture or delivery to industry partners in different countries. The ability to send digital files of information to be 3D printed or manufactured has made huge changes to design and manufacture globally. Art and design students should be aware of the potential that working collaboratively can bring, and should also be aware of the need for excellent communication and presentation skills, and to be able to express ideas visually so that language barriers are easily overcome.

Communication and collaboration are two highly valued skills for employment. The ability to understand or empathise with a client or a working partner can be a key factor in the success of a collaborative project. Being able to meet shared deadlines, and produce work to a required standard on time and on budget, is vital for success in the Art and Design industry, if not every industry.

> **LESSON IDEA 12.2: PARTNERSHIP PROJECTS**
>
> Making links with other schools in different regions can broaden students' understanding of other cultures, and the differences and similarities they each face. A collaborative project over Skype with another school could be a great way of introducing global thinking to a creative project. This could be achieved by partnering with a school in a different country and working on the same project together.
>
> Students could set a brief for each other, for example:
>
> - to make a video diary of your school day
> - to design a school bag for the partner school
> - to paint a postcard about the area you live in and send it to the partner school.
>
> The finished designs and outcomes could be displayed in each other's schools, or as a virtual exhibition on the school websites.

Finding a personal connection can make a global project feel more relevant. This could be:

- a place where the teacher or student originates from
- working to a common goal or common set of competencies; in this case even studying the same syllabus could be the shared experience
- exploring a theme that creates a personal connection; for example, a cultural or environmental issue that a student feels strongly about
- working in partnership with another school from a different place, to explore shared experiences and differences.

Aspiration

Global thinking can help students to understand that they are part of something that extends beyond their home and school. They can feel that other people share the same opinions or concerns, and it can help them to realise that they have the potential to shape the future. It can also be a means of ensuring that students feel that they have a voice and can be heard. Over the years, I've seen some beautiful, well-constructed and thoughtful projects from students who have chosen topics such as global warming or freedom of speech as their starting point.

Sometimes, students also choose challenging topics and use their creativity as a means to explore these difficult topics within a safe environment. Exploring these topics helps students to realise that they are valued and their opinions can be heard, or they might be the voice of someone who cannot speak for themselves for whatever reason. Within your own school, you may have an understanding of what is acceptable or not, and be able to help students to manage an aspirational project and explore boundaries in a safe way, without being overly challenging or offensive.

Intellectual property, copyright and originality

Copyright infringement is a global issue. From the beginning of their course, students need to be taught respect for other people's intellectual property, and the ethical and legal issues around plagiarising images or ideas. It's also important to teach students how to protect their own original ideas.

They should understand the importance of:

- valuing authenticity and their own original creative outcomes
- developing originality in their design ideas
- ensuring that their work is not a copy of someone else's work
- crediting all sources used for reference
- protecting their own ideas and intellectual property.

Teacher Tip

Proving ownership of an idea can be achieved by simple actions, such as adding the date to sketchbook pages and taking photographs of work in progress. Annotating, dating and recording images in sketchbooks can be a way of authenticating a student's own original work. It is good practice for art students to work in this way as they progress through their studies and into employment: if needed, they will be able to demonstrate that a piece of work is their own.

Summary

There are lots of opportunities to include global thinking and broaden students' outlook in Art and Design.

- Encourage projects that use global issues as starting points.

- Explore themes and topics that are relevant or meaningful to the students.

- Use references from artists, designers and other cultures, crediting all sources properly.

- Carefully guide students in their exploration of these themes so that they understand boundaries.

- Embed these broader thinking skills into the assessment – this will demonstrate to students how valuable they are.

- Global thinking skills can be assessed through critical thinking and contextual understanding.

Reflective practice

13

Dr Paul Beedle, Head of Professional Development
Qualifications, Cambridge International

'As a teacher you are always learning'

It is easy to say this, isn't it? Is it true? Are you bound to learn just by being a teacher?

You can learn every day from the experience of working with your students, collaborating with your colleagues and playing your part in the life of your school. You can learn also by being receptive to new ideas and approaches, and by applying and evaluating these in practice in your own context.

To be more precise, let us say that as a teacher:

* you **should** always be learning
  to develop your expertise throughout your career for your own fulfilment as a member of the teaching profession and to be as effective as possible in the classroom.
* you **can** always be learning
  if you approach the teaching experience with an open mind, ready to learn and knowing how to reflect on what you are doing in order to improve.

You want your professional development activities to be as relevant as possible to what you do and who you are, and to help change the quality of your teaching and your students' learning – for the better, in terms of outcomes, and for good, in terms of lasting effect. You want to feel that 'it all makes sense' and that you are actively following a path that works for you personally, professionally and career-wise.

So professional learning is about making the most of opportunities and your working environment, bearing in mind who you are, what you are like and how you want to improve. But simply experiencing – thinking about and responding to situations, and absorbing ideas and information – is not necessarily learning. It is through reflection that you can make the most of your experience to deepen and extend your professional skills and understanding.

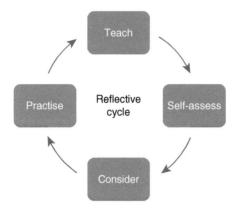

Figure 13.1

In this chapter, we will focus on three *essentials* of reflective practice, explaining in principle and in practice how you can support your own continuing professional development:

1 **Focusing** on what you want to learn about and why.
2 **Challenging** yourself and others to go beyond description and assumptions to critical analysis and evaluation.
3 **Sharing** what you are learning with colleagues – to enrich understanding and enhance the quality of practice.

These essentials will help you as you apply and adapt the rich ideas and approaches in this book in your own particular context. They will also help you if you are, or are about to be, taking part in a Cambridge Professional Development Qualification (Cambridge PDQ) programme, to make the most of your programme, develop your portfolio and gain the qualification.

1 Focus
In principle

Given the multiple dimensions and demands of being a teacher, you might be tempted to try to cover 'everything' in your professional development but you will then not have the time to go beneath the surface much at all. Likewise, attending many different training events will certainly keep you very busy but it is unlikely that these will simply add up to improving your thinking and practice in sustainable and systematic ways.

Teachers who are beginning an organised programme of professional learning find that it is most helpful to select particular ideas, approaches and topics which are relevant to their own situation and their school's priorities. They can then be clear about their professional learning goals, and how their own learning contributes to improving their students' learning outcomes. They deliberately choose activities that help make sense of their practice with their students in their school and have a clear overall purpose.

It is one thing achieving focus, and another maintaining this over time. When the going gets tough, because it is difficult either to understand or become familiar with new ideas and practices, or to balance learning time with the demands of work and life, it really helps to have a mission – to know why you want to learn something as well as what that something is. Make sure that this is a purpose which you feel genuinely belongs to you and in which you have a keen interest, rather than it being something given to you or imposed on you. Articulate your focus not just by writing it down but by 'pitching' it to a colleague whose opinion you trust and taking note of their feedback.

In practice

- Plan
  What is my goal and how will I approach the activity?

  Select an approach that is new to you, but make sure that you understand the thinking behind this and that it is relevant to your students' learning. Do it for real effect, not for show.

- Monitor
  Am I making progress towards my goal; do I need to try a different approach?

  Take time during your professional development programme to review how far and well you are developing your understanding of theory and practice. What can you do to get more out of the experience, for example by discussing issues with your mentor, researching particular points, and asking your colleagues for their advice?

- Evaluate
  What went well, what could have been better, what have I learned for next time?

  Evaluation can sometimes be seen as a 'duty to perform' – like clearing up after the event – rather than the pivotal moment in learning that it really is. Evaluate not because you are told you have to; evaluate to make sense of the learning experience you have been through and what it means to you, and to plan ahead to see what you can do in the future.

This cycle of planning, monitoring and evaluation is just as relevant to you as a professional learner as to your students as learners. Be actively in charge of your learning and take appropriate actions. Make your professional development work for you. Of course your professional development programme leaders, trainers and mentors will guide and support you in your learning, but you are at the heart of your own learning experience, not on the receiving end of something that is cast in stone. Those who assist and advise you on your professional development want you and your colleagues to get the best out of the experience, and need your feedback along the way so that if necessary they can adapt and improve what they are devising.

2 Challenge

In principle

Reflection is a constructive process that helps the individual teacher to improve their thinking and practice. It involves regularly asking questions of yourself about your developing ideas and experience, and keeping track of your developing thinking, for example in a reflective journal. Reflection is continuous, rather than a one-off experience. Being honest with yourself means thinking hard, prompting yourself to go beyond your first thoughts about a new experience and to avoid taking for granted your opinions about something to which you are accustomed. Be a critical friend to yourself.

In the Cambridge PDQ Certificate in Teaching and Learning, for example, teachers take a fresh look at the concepts and processes of learning and challenge their own assumptions. They engage with theory and models of effective teaching and learning, and open their minds through observing experienced practitioners, applying new ideas in practice and listening to formative feedback from mentors and colleagues. To evidence in their assessed portfolio how they have learned from this experience, they not only present records of observed practice but also critical analysis showing understanding of how and why practices work and how they can be put into different contexts successfully.

The Cambridge PDQ syllabuses set out key questions to focus professional learning and the portfolio templates prompts to help you. These questions provide a framework for reflection. They are open-ended and will not only stimulate your thinking but lead to lively group discussion. The discipline of asking yourself and others questions such as 'Why?' 'How do we know?' 'What is the evidence?' 'What are the conditions?' leads to thoughtful and intelligent practice.

In practice

Challenge:

- Yourself, as you reflect on an experience, to be more critical in your thinking. For example, rather than simply describing what happened, analyse why it happened and its significance, and what might have happened if conditions had been different.
- Theory – by understanding and analysing the argument, and evaluating the evidence that supports the theory. Don't simply accept a theory as a given fact – be sure that you feel that the ideas make sense and that there is positive value in applying them in practice.
- Convention – the concept of 'best practice(s)' is as good as we know now, on the basis of the body of evidence, for example on the effect size of impact of a particular approach on learning outcomes (defined in the next chapter). By using an approach in an informed way and with a critical eye, you can evaluate the approach relating to your particular situation.

3 Share

In principle

Schools are such busy places, and yet teachers can feel they are working on their own for long periods because of the intensity of their workload as they focus on all that is involved in teaching their students. We know that a crucial part of our students' active learning is the opportunity to collaborate with their peers in order to investigate, create and communicate. Just so with professional learning: teachers learn best through engagement with their peers, in their own school and beyond. Discussion and interaction with colleagues, focused on learning and student outcomes, and carried out in a culture of openness, trust and respect, helps each member of the community of practice in the school clarify and sharpen their understanding and enhance their practice.

This is why the best professional learning programmes incorporate collaborative learning, and pivotal moments are designed into the programme for this to happen frequently over time: formally in guided learning sessions such as workshops and more informally in opportunities such as study group, teach meets and discussion, both face-to-face and online.

In practice

Go beyond expectations!

In the Cambridge PDQ syllabus, each candidate needs to carry out an observation of an experienced practitioner and to be observed formatively themselves by their mentor on a small number of occasions. This is the formal requirement in terms of evidence of practice within the portfolio for the qualification. The expectation is that these are not the only times that teachers will observe and be observed for professional learning purposes (rather than performance appraisal).

However, the more that teachers can observe each other's teaching, the better; sharing of practice leads to advancement of shared knowledge and understanding of aspects of teaching and learning, and development of agreed shared 'best practice'.

So:

- open your classroom door to observation
- share with your closest colleague(s) when you are trying out a fresh approach, such as an idea in this book
- ask them to look for particular aspects in the lesson, especially how students are engaging with the approach – pose an observation question
- reflect with them after the lesson on what you and they have learned from the experience – pose an evaluation question
- go and observe them as they do the same
- after a number of lessons, discuss with your colleagues how you can build on your peer observation with common purpose (for example, lesson study).
- share with your other colleagues in the school what you are gaining from this collaboration and encourage them to do the same
- always have question(s) to focus observations and focus these question(s) on student outcomes.

Pathways

The short-term effects of professional development are very much centred on teachers' students. For example, the professional learning in a Cambridge PDQ programme should lead directly and quickly to changes in the ways your students learn. All teachers have this at heart – the desire to help their students learn better.

The long-term effects of professional development are more teacher-centric. During their career over, say, 30 years, a teacher may teach many thousand lessons. There are many good reasons for a teacher to keep up-to-date with pedagogy, not least to sustain their enjoyment of what they do.

Each teacher will follow their own career pathway, taking into account many factors. We do work within systems, at school and wider level, involving salary and appointment levels, and professional development can be linked to these as requirement or expectation. However, to a significant extent teachers shape their own career pathway, making decisions along the way. Their pathway is not pre-ordained; there is room for personal choice, opportunity and serendipity. It is for each teacher to judge for themselves how much they wish to venture. A teacher's professional development pathway should reflect and support this.

It is a big decision to embark on an extended programme of professional development, involving a significant commitment of hours of learning and preparation over several months. You need to be as clear as you can be about the immediate and long-term value of such a commitment. Will your programme lead to academic credit as part of a stepped pathway towards Masters level, for example?

Throughout your career, you need to be mindful of the opportunities you have for professional development. Gauge the value of options available at each particular stage in your professional life, both in terms of relevance to your current situation – your students, subject and phase focus, and school – and the future situation(s) of which you are thinking.

Understanding the impact of classroom practice on student progress

14

Lee Davis, Deputy Director for Education,
Cambridge International

14

Introduction

Throughout this book, you have been encouraged to adopt a more active approach to teaching and learning and to ensure that formative assessment is embedded into your classroom practice. In addition, you have been asked to develop your students as meta-learners, such that they are able to, as the academic Chris Watkins puts it, 'narrate their own learning' and become more reflective and strategic in how they plan, carry out and then review any given learning activity.

A key question remains, however. How will you know that the new strategies and approaches you intend to adopt have made a significant difference to your students' progress and learning? What, in other words, has been the impact and how will you know?

This chapter looks at how you might go about determining this at the classroom level. It deliberately avoids reference to whole-school student tracking systems, because these are not readily available to all schools and all teachers. Instead, it considers what you can do as an individual teacher to make the learning of your students visible – both to you and anyone else who is interested in how they are doing. It does so by introducing the concept of 'effect sizes' and shows how these can be used by teachers to determine not just whether an intervention works or not but, more importantly, *how well* it works. 'Effect size' is a useful way of quantifying or measuring the size of any difference between two groups or data sets. The aim is to place emphasis on the most important aspect of an intervention or change in teaching approach – the **size of the effect** on student outcomes.

Consider the following scenario:

Over the course of a term, a teacher has worked hard with her students on understanding 'what success looks like' for any given task or activity. She has stressed the importance of everyone being clear about the criteria for success, before students embark upon the chosen task and plan their way through it. She has even got to the point where students have been co-authors of the assessment rubrics used, so that they have been fully engaged in the intended outcomes throughout and can articulate what is required before they have even started. The teacher is happy with developments so far, but has it made a difference to student progress? Has learning increased beyond what we would normally expect for an average student over a term anyway?

Here is an extract from the teacher's markbook.

Student	Sept Task	Nov Task
Katya	13	15
Maria	15	20
Joao	17	23
David	20	18
Mushtaq	23	25
Caio	25	38
Cristina	28	42
Tom	30	35
Hema	32	37
Jennifer	35	40

Figure 14.1

Before we start analysing this data, we must note the following:

- The task given in September was at the start of the term – the task in November was towards the end of the term.
- Both tasks assessed similar skills, knowledge and understanding in the student.
- The maximum mark for each was 50.
- The only variable that has changed over the course of the term is the approaches to teaching and learning by the teacher. All other things are equal.

With that in mind, looking at Figure 14.1, what conclusions might you draw as an external observer?

You might be saying something along the lines of: 'Mushtaq and Katya have made some progress, but not very much. Caio and Cristina appear to have done particularly well. David, on the other hand, appears to be going backwards!'

What can you say about the class as a whole?

Calculating effect sizes

What if we were to apply the concept of 'effect sizes' to the class results in Figure 13.1, so that we could make some more definitive statements about the impact of the interventions over the given time period? Remember, we are doing so in order to understand the size of the effect on student outcomes or progress.

Let's start by understanding how it is calculated.

An effect size is found by calculating 'the standardised mean difference between two data sets or groups'. In essence, this means we are looking for the difference between two averages, while taking into the account the spread of values (in this case, marks) around those averages at the same time.

As a formula, and from Figure 14.1, it looks like the following:

$$\text{Effect size} = \frac{\text{average class mark (after intervention)} - \text{average class mark (before intervention)}}{\text{spread (standard deviation of the class)}}$$

In words: the average mark achieved by the class *before* the teacher introduced her intervention strategies is taken away from the average mark achieved by the class *after* the intervention strategies. This is then divided by the standard deviation[1] of the class as a whole.

---

[1] The standard deviation is merely a way of expressing by how much the members of a group (in this case, student marks in the class) differ from the average value (or mark) for the group.

Understanding the impact of classroom practice on student progress

Inserting our data into a spreadsheet helps us calculate the effect size as follows:

	A	B	C
1	Student	September Task	November Task
2	Katya	13	15
3	Maria	15	20
4	Joao	17	23
5	David	20	18
6	Mushtaq	23	25
7	Caio	25	38
8	Cristina	28	42
9	Tom	30	35
10	Hema	32	37
11	Jennifer	35	40
12			
13	Average mark	23.8 = AVERAGE (B2:B11)	29.3 = AVERAGE (C2:C11)
14	Standard deviation	7.5 = STDEV (B2:B11)	10.11 = STDEV (C2:C11)

Figure 14.2

Therefore, the effect size for this class $= \dfrac{29.3 - 23.8}{8.8} = 0.62$

But what does this mean?

Interpreting effect sizes for classroom practice

In pure statistical terms, a 0.62 effect size means that the average student mark **after** the intervention by the teacher, is 0.62 standard deviations above the average student mark **before** the intervention.

We can state this in another way: the post-intervention average mark now exceeds 61% of the student marks previously.

Going further, we can also say that the average student mark, post-intervention, would have placed a student in the top four in the class previously. You can see this visually in Figure 14.2 where 29.3 (the class average after the teacher's interventions) would have been between Cristina's and Tom's marks in the September task.

This is good, isn't it? As a teacher, would you be happy with this progress by the class over the term?

To help understand effect sizes further, and therefore how well or otherwise the teacher has done above, let us look at how they are used in large-scale studies as well as research into educational effectiveness more broadly. We will then turn our attention to what really matters – talking about student learning.

Effect sizes in research

We know from results analyses of the Program for International Student Assessment (PISA) and the Trends in International Mathematics and Science Study (TIMMS) that, across the world, a year's schooling leads to an effect size of 0.4. John Hattie and his team at The University of Melbourne reached similar conclusions when looking at over 900 meta-analyses of classroom and whole-school interventions to improve student learning – 240 million students later, the result was an effect size of 0.4 on average for all these strategies.

What this means, then, is that any teacher achieving an effect size of greater than 0.4 is doing better than expected (than the average) over the course of a year. From our earlier example, not only are the students making better than expected progress, they are also doing so in just one term.

Here is something else to consider. In England, the distribution of GCSE grades in Maths and English have standard deviations of between 1.5 and 1.8 grades (A*, A, B, C, etc.), so an improvement of one GCSE grade represents an effect size of between 0.5 and 0.7. This means that, in the context of secondary schools, introducing a change in classroom practice of 0.62 (as the teacher achieved above) would result in an improvement of about one GCSE grade for each student in the subject.

Furthermore, for a school in which 50% of students were previously attaining five or more A*–C grades, this percentage (assuming the effect size of 0.62 applied equally across all subjects and all other things being equal) would rise to 73%.

Now, that's something worth knowing.

What next for your classroom practice? Talking about student learning

Given what we now know about 'effect sizes', what might be the practical next steps for you as a teacher?

Firstly, try calculating 'effect sizes' for yourself, using marks and scores for your students that are comparable, e.g. student performance on key skills in Maths, Reading, Writing, Science practicals, etc. Become familiar with how they are calculated so that you can then start interrogating them 'intelligently'.

Do the results indicate progress was made? If so, how much is attributable to the interventions you have introduced?

Try calculating 'effect sizes' for each individual student, in addition to your class, to make their progress visible too. To help illustrate this, let us return to the comments we were making about the progress of some students in Figure 14.1. We thought Cristina and Caio did very well and we had grave concerns about David. Individual effect sizes for the class of students would help us shed light on this further:

Student	September Task	November task	Individual Effect Size
Katya	13	15	0.22*
Maria	15	20	0.55
Joao	17	23	0.66
David	20	18	-0.22
Mushtaq	23	25	0.22
Caio	25	38	1.43
Cristina	28	42	1.54
Tom	30	35	0.55
Hema	32	37	0.55
Jennifer	35	40	0.55

* The individual 'effect size' for each student above is calculated by taking their September mark away from their November mark and then dividing by the standard deviation for the class – in this case, 8.8.

Figure 14.3

If these were your students, what questions would you now ask of yourself, of your students and even of your colleagues, to help you understand why the results are as they are and how learning is best achieved? Remember, an effect size of 0.4 is our benchmark, so who is doing better than that? Who is not making the progress we would expect?

David's situation immediately stands out, doesn't it? A negative effect size implies learning has regressed. So, what has happened, and how will we draw alongside him to find out what the issues are and how best to address them?

Why did Caio and Cristina do so well, considering they were just above average previously? Effect sizes of 1.43 and 1.54 respectively are significantly above the benchmark, so what has changed from their perspective? Perhaps they responded particularly positively to developing assessment rubrics together. Perhaps learning had sometimes been a mystery to them before, but with success criteria now made clear, this obstacle to learning had been removed.

We don't know the answers to these questions, but they would be great to ask, wouldn't they? So go ahead and ask them. Engage in dialogue with your students, and see how their own ability to discuss their learning has changed and developed. This will be as powerful a way as any of discovering whether your new approaches to teaching and learning have had an impact and it ultimately puts data, such as 'effect sizes', into context.

Concluding remarks

'Effect sizes' are a very effective means of helping you understand the impact of your classroom practice upon student progress. If you change your teaching strategies in some way, calculating 'effect sizes', for both the class and each individual student, helps you determine not just *if* learning has improved, but by *how much*.

They are, though, only part of the process. As teachers, we must look at the data carefully and intelligently in order to understand 'why'. Why did some students do better than others? Why did some not make any progress at all? Use 'effect sizes' as a starting point, not the end in itself.

Ensure that you don't do this in isolation – collaborate with others and share this approach with them. What are your colleagues finding in their classes, in their subjects? Are the same students making the same progress across the curriculum? If there are differences, what might account for them?

In answering such questions, we will be in a much better position to determine next steps in the learning process for students. After all, isn't that our primary purpose as teachers?

Acknowledgements, further reading and resources

This chapter has drawn extensively on the influential work of the academics John Hattie and Robert Coe. You are encouraged to look at the following resources to develop your understanding further:

Hattie, J. (2012) *Visible Learning for Teachers – Maximising Impact on Learning*. London and New York: Routledge.

Coe, R. (2002) *It's the Effect Size, Stupid. What effect size is and why it is important.* Paper presented at the Annual Conference of The British Educational Research Association, University of Exeter, England, 12–14 September, 2002. A version of the paper is available online on the University of Leeds website.

The Centre for Evaluation and Monitoring, University of Durham, has produced a very useful 'effect size' calculator (available from their website). Note that it also calculates a confidence interval for any 'effect size' generated. Confidence intervals are useful in helping you understand the margin for error of an 'effect size' you are reporting for your class. These are particularly important when the sample size is small, which will inevitably be the case for most classroom teachers.

Recommended reading

15

For a deeper understanding of the Cambridge approach, refer to the Cambridge International website (http://www. cambridgeinternational.org/teaching-and-learning) where you will find the following resources:

Implementing the curriculum with Cambridge: a guide for school leaders.

Developing your school with Cambridge: a guide for school leaders.

Education Briefs for a number of topics, such as active learning and bilingual education. Each brief includes information about the challenges and benefits of different approaches to teaching, practical tips, lists of resources.

Getting started with ...These are interactive resources to help explore and develop areas of teaching and learning. They include practical examples, reflective questions, and experiences from teachers and researchers.

For further support around becoming a Cambridge school, visit cambridge-community.org.uk.

The resources in this section can be used as a supplement to your learning, to build upon your awareness of Art & Design teaching and the pedagogical themes in this series.

There are several websites and journals that I use regularly to keep up to date with teaching and learning trends and research. One of my areas of interest at the moment is the digital classroom, and how digital equipment and resources are changing the Art and Design classroom.

Chapters 3-10

Ellis, S. and Barrs, M. (2008). The assessment of creative learning. In: J. Sefton-Green, ed., *Creative Learning*, 1st ed. [online] London: Arts Council England., pp.73-89. This is a collection of research findings that cover a range of issues surrounding Art and Design education. It's co-published by the Arts Council England and Creative Partnerships, and it is available online on the Creative Partnerships website. It has some interesting observations about the challenges and opportunities related to teaching creativity, and the extent to which government and education policy can play a role in them.

Lindstom, L. (2006). Creativity: What is it? Can you assess it? Can it be taught? *International Journal of Art & Design Education*, **25**(1), 53–66. This article is a study of teaching visual arts in Sweden and explores ways of building a culture of learning that harnesses creativity, independent learning and self-assessment. It can be accessed via The Wiley Online Library.

Chapter 10 Inclusive education

The BBC Active website has an informative range of up-to-date teaching and learning resources. Some of the topics I found most useful related to teaching with digital technologies and teaching introverts. The Digital Teacher website is also very interesting and useful for international teachers.

Chapter 11 Teaching with digital technologies

Jisc is a company that focuses on providing digital solutions for education and educational research institutions. They have conducted extensive research on the impact of digital resources on teaching and learning. I found some of their case studies very interesting, especially one of the studies about the value of feedback to students via e-portfolios rather than face-to-face. See the Jisc website for further information.

The following is useful on presentations:

Duarte, N. (2008) *Slide:ology: The Art and Science of Creating Great Presentations*. Sebastopol: O'Reilly Media.

Chapter 12 Global thinking

Boix Mansilla, B. and Jackson, A. (2011). *Educating for global competence: preparing our youth to engage the world*. New York: Asia Society. This is available online on the Asia Society website.

Chapter 14 Understanding the impact of classroom practice on student progress

Watkins, C. (2015) *Meta-Learning in Classrooms*. The SAGE Handbook of Learning. Edited by Scott D. and Hargreaves E. London: Sage Publications.

Index

Note: Letters 'f', and 't' following locators refer to figures and tables respectively